Coaching YMCA
Rookies Soccer

YYOUTH SUPER SPORTS.

We build strong kids, strong families, strong communities.

Library of Congress Cataloging-in-Publication Data

Coaching YMCA Rookies soccer / YMCA of the USA.
    p.   cm.
   Includes bibliographical references (p.   )
   ISBN 0-7360-0338-X
   1. Soccer for children--Coaching.   I. YMCA of the USA.
   GV944.2.C63   1999   99-15051
   796.334'07'7--dc21   CIP

ISBN: 0-7360-0338-X

Published for the YMCA of the USA by Human Kinetics Publishers, Inc. Item no.: Y5488
Copyright ©1999 National Council of Young Men's Christian Associations of the United States of
America

Material in chapter 9 and on pages 22–24 and 146–147 is adapted, by permission, from American
Sport Education Program, 1995, *Coaching Youth Soccer,* 2d ed. (Champaign, IL: Human Kinetics).
Material on pages 142–144 is adapted, by permission, from R. Martens, 1997, *Successful Coaching,*
Updated 2d ed. (Champaign, IL: Human Kinetics). Material on pages 148–156 is adapted, by permission, from M.J. Flegel, 1997, *Sport First Aid,* Updated ed. (Champaign, IL: Human Kinetics).

YMCA Project Coordinator: Richard Jones
YMCA Curriculum Consultant: Steve Mitchell
Content Consultant: Karen Partlow
Fitness and Character Development Consultant: Kathleen Madden
Project Writer: Patricia Sammann
Managing Editor: Coree Schutter
Assistant Editor: John Wentworth
Copyeditor: Denelle Eknes
Proofreader: Joanna Hatzopoulos
Graphic Designer: Robert Reuther
Graphic Artist: Francine Hamerski
Photo Editor: Clark Brooks
Cover Designer: Jack W. Davis
Photographer (cover): © Richard Cummins/PHOTOPHILE
Photographers (interior): Tom Roberts, unless otherwise noted; p. 1 © Photo Network; pp. 3, 17,
   33, 75, 119, and 157 © Mary E. Messenger; pp. 13, 19, 27, and 133 © Terry Wild; p. 25 © 1999
   Jim West, p. 141 © Frank Armstrong/Photo Network
Illustrators: Mic Greenberg and Sharon Smith (Mac art); Roberto Sabas (line drawings); Dick
   Flood and Timothy Stiles (cartoons)
Printer: United Graphics

Printed in the United States of America   10 9 8 7 6 5 4 3 2 1

Copies of this book may be purchased from the YMCA Program Store, P.O. Box 5076, Champaign,
IL 61825-5076, (800) 747-0089.

The YMCA of the USA does not operate or manage the YMCA Youth Super Sports Program or any of
its components or facilities associated with the program.

Contents

The Job

Thank you for agreeing to be a coach in the YMCA Rookies program of YMCA Youth Super Sports. The job is challenging, but with effort and enthusiasm, you'll find it rewarding. In part I we'll tell you about YMCA Youth Super Sports, the best sports program in America. As we share with you our philosophy about children's sports programs in chapter 1, you'll see why we think YMCA Youth Super Sports is special. In chapter 2 we'll present you with your job description and request that you bring the YMCA philosophy to life as you teach soccer to your young players. Then in chapter 3 we'll describe what it is like to be a young child four to seven years old (in case you've forgotten). This will give you a feel for what your players are capable of understanding and doing.

In chapter 4 we'll describe the way we want you to teach soccer to your players, what we call the games approach. It's not the traditional way adults have taught sports to children, but you'll see why it is a better way—the YMCA way. It's essential that you understand and use this approach, the games approach, to teaching YMCA Rookies soccer.

Our overall objectives in part I are to prepare you to do your job well and to impress upon you the potential influence you can have on the young people you coach. It's your chance to make a difference!

Welcome to YMCA Youth Super Sports

Thank you for agreeing to be a coach in the YMCA Youth Super Sports program. As a YMCA Rookies coach you will introduce a group of young people to the game of soccer. We ask you to not only teach your players the basic skills and rules of the game, but also make learning the game a joyful experience for them. You see, we want them to play soccer not only for this season, but also for many years to come, and we want you to have fun teaching soccer because we'd like you to help us again next season.

Okay, let's get started. In this guide you'll find essential information about teaching soccer the YMCA way. In the next section we'll explain the best sports program in America—YMCA Youth Super Sports, and especially the YMCA Rookies program of which you'll be a part. Next is your job description for being a YMCA Rookies soccer coach, with reminders about how to work with four- to seven-year-olds. Then we'll show you how to teach soccer using the games approach and provide you with a season plan and a complete set of practice plans for four- to five-year-olds and another for six- to seven-year-olds. In the last part we'll explain how to teach the four main components of the soccer season plan: skills and tactics, rules and traditions, fitness and safety, and character development. And throughout the book, Lucky, the YMCA Youth Super Sports mascot, will help illustrate key points. We hope by seeing Lucky on these pages you'll be reminded to keep the fun in your practices and games.

Please read the entire guide carefully and consult it regularly during the season. If your YMCA offers you the opportunity to participate in a YMCA Rookies Soccer Coaches Course, be there. The three and one-half hour course will help you use the games approach to teaching soccer.

Let's look at what YMCA Youth Super Sports is, the YMCA's philosophy of youth sports, and the three parts of YMCA Youth Super Sports: YMCA Rookies, YMCA Winners, and YMCA Champions.

YMCA Youth Super Sports

We've named the program YMCA Youth Super Sports because we're confident it's the best-designed sport program available for young people ages 4 to 16. We built the program by bringing together the knowledge of sport scientists who've spent their careers studying children's sports with the practical wisdom of YMCA youth sport directors who have guided millions of young people through sports programs. Our objective for YMCA Youth Super Sports is to help young people not only become better players, but also become better people. We recognize that not every child can win the contest, but every kid can be a winner in YMCA Youth Super Sports. That's why our motto for the program is "Building Winners for Life."

The YMCA triangle, representing spirit, mind, and body, is the inspiration for the YMCA Youth Super Sports program triangle shown in figure 1.1. YMCA Youth Super Sports is currently designed for five sports—soccer, baseball and softball, basketball, and volleyball—and consists of three programs:

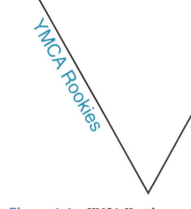

Figure 1.1 YMCA Youth Super Sports triangle.

YMCA Rookies—A precompetitive, instructional program to teach 4- to 7-year-old boys and girls the basic skills and rules of the game.

YMCA Winners—The YMCA's unique, values-based competitive sports program for young people ages 8 to 16.

YMCA Champions—An innovative opportunity for 8- to 16-year-olds to demonstrate personal achievement in and through sport.

All three programs have been carefully crafted to maximize the potential for children to have a positive and beneficial experience under your leadership. We now recognize that sport is not just a frivolous game in children's lives; it has profound influences on them. Through YMCA Youth Super Sports we want to help young people develop character, not become characters. We want to help them learn to *care* about others, to be *honest*, to show *respect*, and to be *responsible*.

Of course, sport doesn't teach these things to young people automatically. What it does is provide them with a good opportunity to learn about and develop these values when volunteer adults like you provide skillful leadership.

YMCA Philosophy of Youth Sports

What we want youth sports to be in the YMCA is stated in our Seven Pillars of YMCA Youth Sports.

◎ **Pillar One—Everyone Plays.** We do not use tryouts to select the best players, nor do we cut kids from YMCA Youth Super Sports. Everyone who registers is assigned to a team. During the season everyone receives equal practice time and plays at least half of every game.

◎ **Pillar Two—Safety First.** Although children may get hurt playing sports, we do all we can to prevent injuries. We've modified each sport to make it safer and more enjoyable to play. We ask you to make sure the equipment and facilities are safe and to teach the sport as we've prescribed so the skills you teach are appropriate for children's developmental level. We ask you to gradually develop your players' fitness levels so they are conditioned for the sport. We also ask you to constantly supervise your young players so you can stop any unsafe activities.

◎ **Pillar Three—Fair Play.** Fair play is about playing by the rules—and more. It's about you and your players showing respect for all who are involved in YMCA Youth Super Sports. It's about you being a role model of sporting behavior and guiding your players to do the same. Remember, we're more interested in developing children's character through sports than in developing a few highly skilled players.

◎ **Pillar Four—Positive Competition.** We believe competition is a positive process when the pursuit of victory remains in the right perspective. The right perspective is when adults make decisions that put the best interests of the children before winning the contest. Learning to compete is important for children, and learning to cooperate in a competitive world is an essential lesson of life. Through YMCA Youth Super Sports we want to help children learn these lessons.

◎ **Pillar Five—Family Involvement.** YMCA Youth Super Sports encourages parents to be involved appropriately in their child's participation in our sports programs. In addition to parents helping as volunteer coaches, officials, and timekeepers, we encourage them to be at practices and games to support their child's participation. To help parents get involved appropriately, YMCA Youth Super Sports offers parent orientation programs.

◎ **Pillar Six—Sport for All.** YMCA Youth Super Sports is an inclusive sport program. That means that children who differ in various characteristics are included in rather than excluded from participation. We offer sports programs for children who differ in physical abilities by matching them with children of similar abilities and modifying the sport. We offer programs to all children regardless of their race, gender, religious creed, or ability. We ask our adult leaders to encourage and appreciate the diversity of children in our society and to encourage the children and their parents to do the same.

◎ **Pillar Seven—Sport for Fun.** Sports are naturally fun for most children. They love the challenge of mastering the skills of the game, playing with their friends, and competing with their peers. Sometimes when adults become involved in children's sports they overorganize and dominate the activity to the point that it destroys children's enjoyment of the sport. If we take the fun out of sports for our children, we are in danger of the kids taking themselves out of sports. Remember the sports are for the kids; let them have fun.

⚽ YMCA Rookies

YMCA Rookies is a skill-development program that prepares children ages four to seven to participate in YMCA Winners, the competitive sports program, and YMCA Champions, the personal sports achievement program. As a coach in YMCA Rookies, we want you to focus on teaching your players the basics of the game in an environment where they can focus on learning the sport, not performing to win.

Too often today children are thrust into competitive sports programs with little instruction on the basics of the sport (both the skills and rules of the game). Perhaps children participate in a few practice sessions, but often they do not obtain sufficient instruction or time to develop basic skills in a precompetitive environment. Then, too, many programs do not sufficiently modify the sport to meet the physical and mental abilities of young children.

The consequence of such an introduction to sports is that children who have had early opportunities for instruction and who are physically more gifted often succeed, but those without these advantages are more likely to fail. We designed YMCA Rookies to address these problems by providing a positive introduction to sports for all children.

To ensure having the highest quality coaches, officials, and sport administrators, YMCA Youth Super Sports offers training and educational resources for all adults involved in YMCA Rookies. The purpose of this training is to emphasize the positive objectives of the program and to de-emphasize the winning-at-all-costs mentality that leads to so many negative practices in youth sports programs.

The training offered to adults involved in the program is just one aspect that makes YMCA Rookies unique. Another is the modifications we've made to the game of soccer so children progress through the program in developmentally appropriate ways. Modifying the game increases the likelihood that children will experience success, and it also reduces the risk of injury.

 YMCA Winners

YMCA Winners is the values-based, competitive program in YMCA Youth Super Sports. It's for young people ages 8 to 16, with the competition typically grouped in two- to three-year age ranges. The objectives of YMCA Winners are the same as those for YMCA Rookies: learning the skills of the game, the rules of the sport, the relationship between fitness and health, and character development. However, in YMCA Winners these objectives are achieved as players compete with other players and teams.

⚽ YMCA Champions

YMCA Champions is an innovative award program that encourages and recognizes personal achievement in YMCA sports among young people ages 8 to 16. As shown in table 1.1, for young people to earn an award they must demonstrate their mastery of the sport in four areas, or domains, and within each sport they have the opportunity to earn three levels of awards.

The four content domains are the following:

1. **Knowledge.** Participants must show that they understand the rules and traditions of the sport and related fitness and health concepts.

2. **Skill.** Young people must demonstrate their mastery of the physical skills of the sport through gamelike skill tests.

3. **Participation.** Young people must participate a certain amount in practices and contests for each of the three levels.

4. **Character.** Participants must demonstrate character development through caring, honesty, respect, and responsibility.

In each sport, participants begin at the Bronze level, the first level of achievement. Once they have obtained the Bronze Award in that sport, they can move on to the Silver and Gold levels. Participants can be working on a Bronze Award in one sport, a Silver Award in another sport, and a Gold Award in a third sport. We encourage them to progress through the levels as rapidly as they wish.

TABLE 1.1

The YMCA Champions Program

| Levels | CONTENT DOMAINS | | | |
	Knowledge	Skill	Participation	Character
Bronze				
Silver				
Gold				

YMCA Champions coaches, who act as mentors for the players, monitor their progress. Gold Leaders, players 14 years old or older who have earned the Gold Award in that sport, assist YMCA Champions coaches. Gold Leaders are trained to assist younger players in their preparation for being tested in the four domains, and they assist the YMCA Champions coaches conducting the evaluations.

Once players have earned a Gold Award, they are eligible to join the YMCA Gold Club. The club is an honorary and service club and provides opportunities for leadership. The Gold Leaders would come from the YMCA Gold Club.

As a YMCA Rookies coach you will play an important role in encouraging young people to participate in both YMCA Winners and YMCA Champions. That encouragement will come not only by urging them to participate, but also by helping them learn the basics of the sport while having fun and building their self-worth.

Your Job Description

N ow you know what YMCA Youth Super Sports is and what our philosophy, or seven pillars, are for conducting this unique sports program. You also know that YMCA Rookies emphasizes teaching children the basic soccer skills and rules in a precompetitive environment. We'll ask you to teach your players how to play the game of soccer, emphasizing teaching, not competing in contests.

Your Duties As a Coach

Here are your seven duties as a YMCA Rookies soccer coach:

1. Teach the skills and tactics of soccer to the best of your ability. We want you to teach children the physical skills and tactics to play the sport to the best of their ability. Kids value learning these skills and tactics, and they respect those who can help them master them. Be a good teacher, but remember that not all children have the same ability to learn. A few have the ability to be outstanding, many to be competent, and a few to barely play the sport. We ask that you help them all be the best they can be.

We'll show you an innovative games approach to teaching and practicing these skills that kids thoroughly enjoy. These games are designed to be developmentally appropriate for the children you will be teaching. You'll avoid monotonous drills in which youngsters stand in line waiting their turn, and instead keep everyone active practicing basic skills in gamelike conditions. To help you, first we'll provide season plans in chapter 5. In chapter 6 we'll give you practice plans for four- to five-year-olds, and in chapter 7 we'll do the same for six- to seven- year-olds. In chapter 8 we'll review how to teach the basic skills and assist you in detecting and correcting errors.

2. **Help your players learn the rules and traditions of soccer.** We'll ask you to teach your players the rules of soccer as they learn the basic skills through the modified games of the sport. Beyond the rules, we'll also ask you to teach the basic traditions of the sport. By traditions we mean the proper actions to show courtesy and avoid injury—in short, to be a good sport. You'll find the rules and traditions for YMCA Rookies soccer in chapter 9.

3. **Help your players become fit and value fitness for a lifetime.** We want you to help your players be fit so they can play soccer safely and successfully. However, we also want more. We want you to do so in a way that your players learn to become fit on their own, understand the value of fitness, and enjoy training. Thus, we ask you not to make them do push-ups or run laps for punishment. Make it fun to get fit for soccer and make it fun to play soccer so they'll stay fit for a lifetime. In chapter 10 we'll give you some tips on basic fitness for your players.

4. **Help young people develop character.** Character development is teaching children the core values—caring, honesty, respect, and responsibility. These intangible qualities are no less important to teach than kicking or defensive skills. We ask you to teach these values to children by conducting team circles, which are built into every practice plan, and demonstrating and encouraging behaviors that express these values at all times. Chapter 11 will give you more suggestions about teaching character development.

5. **Ensure the safety of your players.** You are responsible for supervising every aspect of your players' participation in soccer. Make sure the field is clear of hazardous objects and that the kids do not engage in activities that might injure themselves or others. You have not only a legal but also a moral responsibility to supervise them closely. See chapter 10 for more on safety.

6. **Help each child develop a sense of self-worth.** An essential goal in conducting YMCA Youth Super Sports programs is to help children gain a strong, positive sense of their worth as human beings. For each of us, our most important possession is our self-worth. Please teach our children soccer in a way that helps them grow to respect themselves and others.

7. **Make it fun.** Make learning the game a fantastic positive experience so your players will want to continue playing for many years to come.

Being a Good Coach

Just what makes a good soccer coach?

 A person who knows the sport of soccer well. If you're not familiar with the sport, be sure to attend the YMCA Rookies Soccer Coaches Course and study more about the sport. Refer to the list of useful books and videos in appendix A.

 A person who wants to teach soccer to young people, who cares. Excellent teachers are motivated, have a positive attitude, and give the time to do the job well.

A person who understands young people, who possesses empathy. Empathy is caring about the young people you teach by showing you understand them.

We hope you'll do your best to be a good soccer coach for the children on your team. By doing so, you can help them develop their spirits, minds, and bodies—the goal for all YMCA programs.

Remember They're Kids

One challenge of working with youngsters is that you need to relate to them as children, not as miniature adults. To do this, you must understand where they're coming from—that is, where they are in their development physically, socially, emotionally, and intellectually. What makes it even more challenging is that on any team you coach, you'll likely find early maturers and late bloomers, and this variance applies not only to your group as a whole, but also to each individual. For example, one player may be intellectually mature and quick to understand soccer tactics and skills, but she may be slow in physical development and thus have difficulty in successfully executing the skills. Another may be developed physically but underdeveloped emotionally.

The more familiar you are with the physical capabilities and mindsets of children, the better you'll be able to communicate with them and help them grow through their experience in soccer. The lists on pages 14–18 detail children's development physically, socially, emotionally, and cognitively. Realize that each child will not conform to all the characteristics at any age; this doesn't mean the child is abnormal. These lists provide a general understanding of children's developmental characteristics. Although we can't take you back to when you were four to seven, we can help you remember what it was like—and help you better understand and relate to children.

⚽ Four- to Five-Year-Olds

Physical Characteristics

At Four

◎ Children's running, jumping, hopping, throwing, and catching become better coordinated.

◎ They are able to gallop and skip on one foot.

◎ They can ride a tricycle.

At Five

◎ Children are three and one-half to three and three-quarter feet tall. They may grow from two to three inches and gain from three to six pounds during the year.

◎ Girls may be about a year ahead of boys in physiological development.

◎ Children are beginning to have better body control.

◎ Their large muscles are better developed than the small muscles that control the fingers and hands.

◎ Their eye and hand coordination is not yet complete.

◎ Children are vigorous and noisy, but their activity appears to have a definite direction.

◎ They tire easily and need plenty of rest.

Social Characteristics

At Four

◎ Children form their first friendships.

◎ They are becoming less likely to play alone and more likely to play interactively with others.

At Five

◎ Children are interested in neighborhood games with other children. They sometimes play games to test their skill.

Development characteristics are adapted from the following:

Berk, Laura E. *Development Through the Lifespan.* Copyright © 1993 by Allyn & Bacon. Adapted by permission.

Humphrey, James H. *Sports for Children: A Guide for Adults.* Copyright © by Charles C Thomas, Publisher, Ltd. Adapted by permission.

◎ They like being with other children, and they seem to get along best in small groups.

◎ Their interests are largely self-centered.

◎ Children imitate when they play.

◎ They get along well in taking turns and they respect others' belongings.

◎ Children show an interest in home activities.

Emotional Characteristics

At Four

◎ Self-conscious emotions (shame, embarrassment, guilt, envy, and pride) become more common.

At Five

◎ Children seldom show jealousy toward younger siblings.

◎ Children usually see only one way to do things and one answer to a question.

◎ They are inclined not to change plans in the middle of an activity; instead, they'd rather start over.

◎ They may fear being deprived of their mothers.

◎ They are learning to get along better, but they still may resort to quarreling and fighting.

◎ They like to be trusted with errands and enjoy performing simple tasks. They want to please and to do what you expect of them.

◎ They can better interpret, predict, and influence others' emotional reactions.

◎ They are beginning to sense right and wrong in terms of specific situations.

Cognitive Characteristics

At Four

◎ They can generalize remembered information from one situation to another.

◎ They have a basic understanding of causality in familiar situations.

At Five

◎ They enjoy copying designs, letters, and numbers and counting objects.

◎ They are interested in completing tasks.

◎ Their memory for past events is good.

◎ They are able to plan activities.

◎ These children may tend to monopolize table conversation.

◎ They look at books and pretend to read.

◎ They like recordings, words, and music that tell stories. They also enjoy stories, dramatic plays, and poems.

◎ Children of this age can sing simple melodies, beat good rhythms, and recognize simple tunes. They enjoy making up dances to music.

◎ Their daydreams seem to center around make-believe play.

◎ They have over 2,000 words in their speaking vocabularies and their pronunciation is usually clear. They can speak in complete sentences and can express their needs well in words.

◎ Their attention span may have increased up to 20 minutes in some cases.

 ## Six- to Seven-Year-Olds

Physical Characteristics

At Six

◎ Children are three and one-half to four feet tall and grow gradually.

◎ They usually have a lot of energy.

◎ They like to move, doing things such as running, jumping, chasing, and playing dodging games.

◎ Their muscular control is becoming more effective with large objects.

◎ A noticeable change occurs in eye-hand coordination. Children can tie their shoes and write their names.

◎ Children's legs are lengthening rapidly.

At Seven

◎ They may grow two to three inches and gain three to five pounds during the year.

◎ They may tire easily and show fatigue in the afternoon.

◎ Whole-body movements are under better control.

◎ Children can throw better and catch more accurately.

◎ Children's reaction times are slow.

◎ Eye-hand coordination improves.

◎ Children's hearts and lungs are smallest in proportion to their body size.

◎ Children may be susceptible to disease and have low resistance.

◎ Children's endurance is low.

◎ Small accessory muscles are developing.

Social Characteristics

At Six

◎ These children are self-centered and need praise.

◎ They like to be first.

◎ Sex differences are not of great importance to them at this age.

◎ They enjoy group play when groups are small.

◎ Children like parties, but their behavior may not always be proper.

◎ Most of them like school and have a desire to learn.

◎ They are interested in the conduct of their friends.

◎ They show an interest in group approval.

At Seven

◎ They want recognition for individual achievements.

◎ They are not always good losers.

◎ They often talk about their families.

◎ They are interested in friends and are not influenced by friends' social or economic status.

◎ They begin to learn to stand up for their rights.

◎ Some children may have nervous habits, such as nail biting, tongue sucking, scratching, or pulling on the ear.

◎ Children are beginning to have a sense of time.

◎ Children show signs of being cooperative.

Emotional Characterisitcs

At Six

◎ Their anger may be difficult to control at times.

◎ Their behavior may often be explosive and unpredictable.

◎ Sometimes children show jealousy toward siblings, but at other times the children take pride in them.

◎ They are greatly excited by anything new.

◎ They may be self-assertive and dramatic.

At Seven

◎ They have learned more control over anger.

◎ They become less impulsive and boisterous than at six.

◎ Their curiosity and creative desires may condition their responses.

◎ Children are critical of themselves and sensitive to failure. It may be difficult for them to take criticism from adults, and they are overanxious to reach the goals set for them by parents and teachers.

◎ Children want to be more independent. They reach for new experiences and try to relate to a larger world.

Cognitive Characteristics

At Six

◎ They have a speaking vocabulary of over 2,500 words.

◎ Their interest span is likely to be short.

◎ They know number combinations up to 10 and the comparative values of common coins.

◎ They can define objects in terms of what they are used for.

◎ They know the right and left sides of the body.

◎ Their drawings are crude, but realistic.

◎ They will contribute to guided group planning.

◎ Their conversations usually are concerned with their own experiences and interests.

◎ These children's curiosity is active, and their memory is strong.

◎ They identify with imaginary characters.

At Seven

◎ Their attention span is still short, but they do not object to repetition. They can listen longer at seven than at six.

◎ Their reaction time is still slow.

◎ They are becoming more realistic and less imaginative.

◎ They can read some books themselves.

◎ They can reason, but they have little experience upon which to base their judgments.

◎ They can barely begin to think abstractly.

◎ They are learning to evaluate the achievements of themselves and others.

◎ They are concerned with their own lack of skill and achievement.

The Games Approach to Teaching Soccer

Do you remember as a kid how adults taught you to play a sport, either in an organized sport program or physical education class? They probably taught you the basic skills using a series of drills that, if the truth be known, you found boring. As you began to learn the basic skills, they eventually taught you the tactics of the game, showing you when to use these skills in various game situations. Do you remember how impatient you became during what seemed to be endless instruction, and how much you just wanted to play? Well, forget this traditional approach to teaching sports.

Now can you recall learning a sport by playing with a group of your friends in the neighborhood? You didn't learn the basic skills first; there was no time for that. You began playing immediately. If you didn't know the basic things to do, your friends told you quickly during the game so they could keep playing. Try to remember, because we're going to ask you to use a very similar approach to teaching soccer to young people. It's called the games approach, an approach we think knocks the socks off the traditional method.

On the surface, it would seem to make sense to introduce soccer by first teaching the basic skills of the sport, then the tactics of the game, but we've discovered that this approach has two serious shortcomings. First, it teaches the skills of the sport out of the context of the game. Kids may learn to control, kick, pass, and dribble the ball, but they find it difficult to use these skills within the game because they don't understand the tactics of the game.

Second, learning skills by doing drills outside of the context of the game is so-o-o-o boring. The single biggest turnoff about adults teaching kids sports is that we overorganize the instruction and deprive kids of their intrinsic desire to play the game.

As a YMCA Rookies coach we're asking that you teach soccer the YMCA way, the games approach way. Clear the traditional approach out of your mind. Once you fully understand the games approach, you'll quickly see its superiority in teaching soccer. The kids will not only learn the game better, but you and they will have much more fun. As a bonus, you'll have far fewer discipline problems.

With the games approach, all teaching of soccer skills begins by playing the game, usually a modified version of the game for younger children. As the children play the game, you help them learn what to do, what we call *tactical awareness*. When your players understand what they must do in the game, they are then eager to develop the skills to play the game. Once players are motivated to learn the skills, you can demonstrate the skills of the game, have players practice using gamelike drills, and provide individual instruction by identifying players' errors and helping to correct them.

In the traditional approach to teaching sports, players do this:

Learn the skill → **Learn the tactics** → **Play the game**

In the games approach players do this:

Play the game → **Learn the tactics** → **Learn the skill**

In the past we have placed too much emphasis on the learning of skills and not enough on learning how to play skillfully—that is, how to use those skills during play. The games approach, in contrast, emphasizes learning what to do first, then how to do it. Moreover—and this is important—the games approach lets kids discover what to do in the game, not by you telling them, but by them experiencing it. What you do as an effective coach is help them discover what they've experienced.

In contrast to the "skill-drill-kill the enthusiasm" approach, the games approach is a guided discovery method of teaching. It empowers your kids to solve the problems that arise in the game, and that's a big part of the fun in learning a game.

Now let's look more closely at the games approach to see the four-step process for teaching soccer:

1. Play a modified soccer game.

2. Help the players discover what they need to do to play the game successfully.

3. Teach the skills of the game.

4. Practice the skills in another game.

Step 1. Play a Modified Soccer Game

Okay, it's the first day of practice; some kids are eager to start, while others are obviously apprehensive. Some have rarely kicked a ball, most don't know the rules, and none know the positions in soccer. What do you do?

If you use the traditional approach, you start with a little warm-up activity, then line the players up for a simple kicking drill and go from there. With the games approach, you begin by playing a modified game that is developmentally appropriate for the level of the players and also designed to focus on learning a specific part of the game.

Don't worry about modifying the game to be developmentally appropriate—we've done it for you. Our practice plans in part II are based on three-player teams for four- to five-year-olds and four-player teams for six- to seven-year-olds. We've also modified the size of the field, the goal, the ball, and the rules. We'll tell you more about these changes later.

The second reason to modify the game is to place emphasis on a limited number of situations in the game. This is one way you guide your players to discover certain tactics in the game.

For instance, you have your players play a 3 v 3 (three players versus three players) game, making the objective of the game to keep the ball away from the other team and score. Playing the game forces players to think about what they have to do to keep the ball and score.

Step 2. Help the Players Discover What They Need to Do

As your players are playing the game, look for the right spot to "freeze" the action, step in, and hold a brief question-and-answer session to discuss problems they were having in carrying out the goal of the game. You don't need to pop in on the first miscue, but if they repeat the same types of mental or physical mistakes a few times in a row, step in and ask them questions that relate to the goal of the game and the necessary skills required. The best time to interrupt the game is when you notice that they are having trouble carrying out the main goal, or aim, of the game. By stopping the game, freezing action, and asking questions, you'll help them understand

- ◎ what is the aim of the game;
- ◎ what they must do to achieve that aim; and
- ◎ what skills they must use to achieve that aim.

After you've discussed the aim, you can begin the skill practice.

Here's an example of how to use questions in the games approach, continuing the example of the modified game we used earlier. Your players just played a game in which the objective was to keep the ball and score. You see that they are having trouble doing this, so you interrupt the action and ask the following questions:

Coach: How can you keep the ball as a team?
Players: Pass.

Coach: What do you need to do in addition to passing?
Players: Receive and control.

Coach: If a player with the ball wants to pass, what does he or she need? (You may need to set this up in a demonstration.)
Players: Someone to pass to.

Through the modified game and skillful questioning on your part, your players realize that receiving and controlling the ball are essential to their success. Just as important, rather than TELLING them that these skills are critical, you led them to that discovery through a well-designed modified game and through questions. This questioning that leads to players' discovery is a crucial part of the games approach. Essentially you'll be asking your players—usually literally—"What do you need to do to succeed in this situation?"

Asking the right questions is an important part of your teaching. We've given you sample questions in each practice plan (see chapters 6 and 7) to help you know where to begin. At first, asking questions will be difficult because your players have so little experience with the game. Also, if you've learned sports through the traditional approach, you'll be tempted to tell your players how to play the game and not waste time asking them questions. Resist this powerful temptation to tell them what to do, and especially don't tell them before they begin to play the game.

If your players have trouble understanding what to do, phrase your questions to let them choose between one option and another. For example, if you ask them "What's the fastest way to get the ball down the field?" and get answers such as "Throw it" or "Hit it," then ask "Is it passing or dribbling?"

Sometimes players simply need to have more time playing the game, or you may need to make a further modification to the game so it is even easier for them to discover what they are to do. It'll take more patience on your part, but it's a powerful way to learn. Don't be reluctant to change the numbers in the teams or some aspect of the structure of the game to aid this discovery. In fact, we advocate playing "lopsided" games (such as 3 v 1 or 3 v 2) in the second game of each practice; we'll explain this concept in a moment.

Step 3. Teach the Skills of the Game

Only when your players recognize the skills they need to be successful in the game do you want to teach the specific skills through focused drills. Now you can use the more traditional approach to teaching sports skills, called IDEA:

I Introduce the skill.

D Demonstrate the skill.

E Explain the skill.

A Attend to players practicing the skill.

Let's take a look at each part of the approach.

Introduce the Skill

Your players will already have some idea of what the skill is you want to teach because they've tried it during a game and talked about it. This is an opportunity to get them focused on the specific skill. You can do this in three ways:

◎ **First, get their attention.** Make sure your players are all positioned where they can see and hear you, and ask them if they can before you begin. Be sure they are not facing the sun or some other distraction. When you speak, be enthusiastic, talk slightly louder than normal, and look your players in the eye.

◎ **Next, name the skill.** If the skill is referred to by more than one name, choose one and stick with it. This helps prevent confusion and makes it easier for you and your players to communicate.

◎ **Finally, briefly review how the skill will help them in the game.** They should have some idea from your earlier questioning, but make sure they see how it fits in the game and describe how the skill relates to more advanced skills.

Demonstrate the Skill

Players, especially young ones, can learn a lot more from seeing the skill performed than just hearing about it. It's important that the skill be shown correctly, so if you don't feel you can demonstrate it well, have another adult or a skilled player do it. Here are some tips on demonstrating a skill:

◎ Use correct form.

◎ Demonstrate the skill several times.

◎ During one or two performances, slow the action so players can see every movement involved in the skill.

◎ Perform the skill at different angles so your players can get a full perspective on it.

◎ Demonstrate the skill with both the right and the left legs.

Explain the Skill

Help your players understand what they see in the demonstration by giving them a short and simple explanation. Relate the skill to previously learned ones, when possible.

To see if your explanation is working, ask your players whether they understand it. A good way to do this is to have them repeat the explanation to you. Ask questions like "What are you going to do first?" "Then what?" and watch for players who look confused or uncertain. Try to explain the skill using different words, which may give players a different perspective.

Because you are working with young children who have short attention spans, take no more than 3 minutes to do the introduction, demonstration, and explanation. Follow it immediately with practice.

Attend to Players Practicing the Skill

The practice plans found in chapters 6 and 7 will provide you with specific ideas on how to run the practice, as well as cue words you should use during practice. Use these cues to help children remember what to focus on during practice.

As your players practice, watch them closely to see which ones can use additional help. Some children will need you to physically guide them through the skill; doing this will help them gain the confidence they need to try. Most will just need some feedback from you, and they'll be glad to get it—if you do it the right way.

Nobody likes to be yelled at, especially when they're supposed to be having fun! The young children you are working with have little or no prior experience with soccer, or even sports in general. They also have not fully developed their motor skills, so you should expect to see more incorrect than correct movements during practice. If you lose your cool when a player makes a mistake, you're just teaching that player to stop trying or to get upset about errors—not exactly what you had in mind. Let your players know that making mistakes isn't the end of the world.

If you have to correct a player, be sure you don't follow a positive statement with the word *but.* For example, don't say "Alesha, your dribbling is great, but you're playing way too close to the other players." Saying it this way causes many kids to ignore the positive statement and focus on the negative one. Instead of the word *but,* use the word *and.* Say something like "Alesha, your dribbling is great, and now let's work on you getting into open space on the field."

Praise from you is very motivational for your players. Be sure to tell them what they are doing right as well as help them correct what they are doing wrong.

⚽ Step 4. Practice the Skills in Another Game

Once the players have practiced the skill, you then put them in another game situation—this time a lopsided game (such as 3 v 1 or 3 v 2). Why use lopsided teams? It's simple: as a coach, you want your players to experience success as they're learning skills. The best way to experience success early on is to create an advantage for the players. This makes it more likely that, for instance, in a 3 v 1 game, your three offensive players will be able to make four passes before attempting to score.

When you get to the practice plans in chapters 6 and 7, you'll see that we often use even-sided games (such as 3 v 3 or 4 v 4) in the first games and lopsided games in the second games. The reasoning behind this is to first introduce players to a situation similar to what they will experience in competition and let them discover the challenges they face in performing the necessary skill. Then you teach them the skill, have them practice it, and put them back in another game—this time a lopsided one to give them a greater chance of experiencing success.

As players improve their skills, you don't need to use lopsided games. At a certain point having a 3 v 1 or 4 v 1 advantage will be too easy for the kids and won't challenge them to hone their skills. At that point you lessen the advantage to, say, 3 v 2 or 4 v 3, or you may even decide that they're ready to practice the skill in even-sided competition. The key is to set up situations where your players experience success, yet are challenged in doing so. This will take careful monitoring on your part, but having kids play lopsided games as they are learning skills is a very effective way of helping them learn and improve.

So, that's the games approach. Your players will get to *play* more in practice, and once they learn how the skill fits in with their performance and enjoyment of the game, they'll be more motivated to work on those skills, which will help them to be successful.

Part II

The Coaching Plans

Now you understand what your job is as a coach, especially the games approach to teaching soccer that we want you to use. In this part we'll map out what we want you to teach players. In chapter 5 we'll present the season plans for what you'll teach the entire season, not only the skills and tactics but also the rules and traditions, the fitness concepts, and a few key character development concepts. Then in chapter 6 we will provide you with 10 practice plans for four- and five-year-olds, and in chapter 7, 10 practice plans for six- to seven-year-olds. When you want to know more about how to teach a skill, a rule, or a fitness or character concept listed in the practice plans, you'll find it in part III.

The Season Plans

If you're feeling a bit overwhelmed by the job you've taken on, here's where we offer specific guidance on what to teach. This chapter will give you an overview of the season plans for each of the two age groups; separate chapters of practice plans for each group will follow.

The season plans we've laid out have five components:

◎ Purpose

◎ Tactics and skills

◎ Rules and traditions

◎ Fitness concepts

◎ Character development concepts

Here's a brief description of each component:

◎ **Purpose.** This is the overall purpose of the particular practice—what you are focusing on for that practice.

◎ **Tactics and skills.** Tactics are what to do during the game (and when to do it), an understanding of the problems faced by each team during the game, and how to solve those problems. Ways to maintain possession of the ball would be tactics. Skills are the physical skills traditionally taught, such as passing or shooting the ball, or controlling the ball during play.

◉ **Rules and traditions.** Here, you teach the rules of the sport to young children gradually, as part of playing games and learning skills. Traditions are those unwritten rules that players follow to be courteous and safe, such as raising your hand when you foul someone or playing cooperatively with the others on your team.

◉ **Fitness concepts.** Even young children can understand simple fitness concepts, such as the idea that exercise strengthens your heart, so we suggest some as the focus for brief discussions during practice.

◉ **Character development concepts.** You can relate the four core values—caring, honesty, respect, and responsibility—to many situations that arise while playing soccer. For example, playing cooperatively with teammates shows that you care about them. Again, we'll suggest specific ideas for briefly discussing character development values.

 ## Season Plan for Four- to Five-Year-Olds

At this age, children need understanding and skills to enable them to play a game. Tactically, this means helping them see the need to keep the ball and to attack the goal, and also to try to stop their opponents from scoring. The following overview provides a weekly guide and shows tactical and skill components we address, along with the rules and traditions and the fitness and character development concepts that we will detail in the practice plans.

Four- to Five-Year-Olds

Week	Purpose	Tactics and skills	Rules and traditions	Fitness concepts	Character development concepts
1	Playing the 3 v 3 game—boundaries, rules	Starting and restarting the game Scoring into the goal	Start and restart rules (no throw-ins yet) Modified boundaries	**General fitness** Participation in sport improves fitness.	**Four core values** The four core values are introduced.
2	Playing the 3 v 3 game under control	Dribbling under control—keeping the ball close; using the inside and outside of the foot	Rule—No use of hands on the field!	**Cardiorespiratory fitness** Your heart is a muscle.	**Responsibility to others** Players should stay under control.
3	Playing the 3 v 3 game as a team	Passing with the inside of the foot Passing in a game Partner passing practice—stationary and moving		**Muscular strength and endurance** Playing soccer strengthens leg muscles.	**Honesty** If you foul, raise your hand and tell the coach.
4	Keeping possession of the ball	Passing and receiving Receiving and dribbling under pressure in a game		**Safety equipment and rules** Wear proper safety equipment.	**Caring** Take turns with teammates.
5	Keeping possession of the ball as a team	Supporting the team-mate with the ball—being in position to "help"	Soccer is a team sport—all players on the team work together.	**Healthy habits** Eat nutritious foods and get enough sleep.	**Caring** Support teammates when they make a mistake.
6	Keeping possession in the game	Passing, receiving, and supporting under pressure		**Flexibility** Stretching makes muscles more flexible.	**Responsibility** It's important that everyone work hard during practice.
7	Attacking the goal	Shooting at the goal—stationary and moving ball		**Muscular strength and endurance** Your leg muscles get stronger when you practice kicking.	**Respect** Be respectful to opponents.
8	Attacking the goal in the game	Shooting at the goal—moving ball under pressure		**Training and conditioning** Being active outside of practice. is important.	**Responsibility** Share team duties with the coach.
9	Defending space	Marking (guarding) opposing players—where to stand, following the opponent	Marking means guarding your opponent.	**Muscular strength and endurance** Practicing kicking strengthens thigh muscles.	**Respect for your opponent** Shake hands with opponents at the end of a game.
10	Defending your own space in the game	Moving to challenge for the ball Pressuring the ball carrier		**Healthy habits** List and discuss healthy habits.	**Keeping perspective on the game** Learn and have fun while playing.

Season Plan for Six- to Seven-Year-Olds

Using a small number of players on a team with the 4 v 4 game allows players to have many tactical options without the pressure of large numbers of opponents. This makes it more likely that players will attempt to pass, dribble, or shoot as the need arises, rather than simply kicking the ball away as far as possible. Progressing from the four- to five-year-old age group, players can now revisit the tactical components of possession and attack while adding a closer look at defending. The following overview provides a weekly guide that shows the tactical and skill components we address, along with the other types of activities described previously. We will detail these in the practice plans. Boys and girls should still play together at this age level.

Six- to Seven-Year-Olds

Week	Purpose	Tactics and skills	Rules and traditions	Fitness concepts	Character development concepts
1	Playing the 4 v 4 game—boundaries, rules	Starting and restarting the games—kicking off, throwing in from out-of-bounds, restarting at corners Scoring into the goal	Rules—starts and restarts, corner kicks, goal kicks, throw-ins, scoring rules Modified boundaries	**General fitness** Participation in sport improves fitness.	**Four core values** The four core values are introduced.
2	Playing the 4 v 4 game as a team	Playing positional and support roles Passing in the game—partner and team practices, and under pressure	Rules—fouls, including no use of hands on the field	**Flexibility** Your muscles need to stretch.	**Responsibility** Learn the team motto: play hard, play fair, and have fun!
3	Keeping possession of the ball	Passing in the game Passing and receiving under pressure Passing and supporting		**Cardiorespiratory fitness** The heart is a special muscle that pumps blood.	**Responsibility** It's important to be a good sport.
4	Keeping possession of the ball in the game	Receiving under pressure Stopping the ball—using the inside and outside of the foot to set up play Receiving and passing, dribbling, shooting under control	Fouls—no hitting, kicking, tripping, pushing, charging or jumping at another player.	**Cardiorespiratory fitness** Your heartbeat increases with exercise.	**Honesty** Raise your hand when you foul.
5	Keeping possession of the ball and attacking as a team	Supporting teammates with the ball Depth in attack		**Cardiorespiratory fitness** Your heart gets stronger when you exercise and play.	**Responsibility** Mistakes are okay. Don't make excuses for your play.
6	Keeping possession and attacking in the game	Passing and receiving Dribbling under pressure Pushing and running		**Flexibility** Stretching muslces makes them flexible.	**Caring** Take turns with teammates.
7	Attacking the goal in the game	Shooting at the goal—good technique under pressure		**Muscular strength and endurance** Running and kicking give you strong legs.	**Responsibility** Keep control of yourself during practice and games.
8	Defending your own space in the game	Marking opposing players—where to stand, following the opponents	Marking means guarding your opponent.	**General fitness** We need to keep active every day, even days we have no practice.	**Responsibility to team** It's important to value teamwork.
9	Defending your own space and winning the ball in the game	Challenging for the ball—tackling	Tackling means taking the ball away from the ball carrier with your feet.	**General fitness** Healthy eating habits give you more energy.	**Caring** Forgive mistakes; they are part of the game.
10	Defending your own space and winning the ball in the game	Marking, pressuring, and tackling		**General fitness** Eat good foods rather than junk foods.	**Respect for game** Realize it takes years to master some skills.

31

Practice Plans for Four- to Five-Year-Olds

This chapter contains 10 practice plans to use with your four- to five-year-old YMCA Rookies soccer players. The plans are based on a 3 v 3 game with simple rules for scoring and starting and restarting the game. Unless otherwise stated, the field should be approximately 30 yards long and 20 yards wide, with a goal about 4 feet high and 8 feet wide. Include no goalkeepers in these games, and use a size 3 ball. Encourage players to obtain and wear shin guards.

This game format is fun, provides each child with many opportunities to play the ball without undue pressure, and teaches the concept of playing within a boundary, thereby forcing players to try to control the ball. Having small teams is crucial at this stage, as it gives children the opportunity to have the ball without a large mob around them. This makes it less likely that they will simply kick the ball away as far as possible.

Let's look briefly at how each plan is organized, then consider a few ideas to make practice organization easy for you.

Each plan contains the following sections:

◉ Purpose

◉ Equipment

◉ Practice Plan

◉ Coach's Points

◉ Variations

Purpose focuses on what you want to teach your players during that practice; it is your main theme for the day. *Equipment* notes what you'll need on hand for that practice. We'll address the *practice plan* in depth in just a moment. *Coach's points* are helpful reminders for you, points of emphasis to most effectively conduct the practice. We include *variations* to games at the end of each plan, providing you with modifications to keep skill practices and games fun and interesting and to help players of varying skill levels.

The practice plan section outlines what you will do during each practice session. It consists of these elements:

◉ Warm-Up

◉ Fitness Circle

◉ Game 1

◉ Skill Practices or Games

◉ Team Circle and Wrap-Up

You'll begin each session with 5- to 10-minute warm-up activities. (*Note:* All times given in the practice plans are approximate.) Follow this with 5 minutes of the fitness circle, during which you briefly talk with players and lead them in an activity that relates to health or fitness. Then, in game 1, you'll be working on the first two steps of the four-step process for teaching soccer: playing a modified soccer game and helping them discover what they need to do. We designed the game to focus players' attention on a particular aspect of soccer. Start the game but, when it's clear that the players are having trouble achieving the goal of the game, stop the game and ask questions and get answers similar to those shown in the plans. The questions and answers will help the players see what skills they need to solve tactical problems in the game. (Occasionally, when the question-and-answer section precedes the coach's cue, ask the questions *before* the players begin the game and use the cue during the game.)

The third part of the four-step process is teaching the skills identified in game 1 through the skill practices. In each skill practice you'll use the IDEA approach to

◎ introduce the skill,

◎ demonstrate the skill,

◎ explain the skill, and

◎ attend to players practicing the skill.

Chapter 8 contains descriptions of all the skills, so we will give a page reference to guide you to the appropriate description. The introduction, demonstration, and explanation should be brief, to fit young children's short attention spans. Then, as the players practice, you will attend to individual children and guide them with coaching cues or further demonstration.

After the skill practices, you will finish the four-step process by having the children play another game. This lets them use the skills they just learned and to develop their understanding of how to use those skills in the context of a game. Note that in game 1, when players are being introduced to a new tactic or skill, they usually will play an even-sided game (such as 3 v 3). This allows them to encounter the challenges they will face in executing the tactic or skill. Then, in most game 2s, they play lopsided games (such as 3 v 1 or 3 v 2) to increase their chances of experiencing success and beginning to master the new tactic or skill. However, if your players are showing proficiency with the new tactic or skill, you can use even-sided games in game 2. The choice is yours; for more on this issue, see chapter 4.

The practice plan section concludes with the team circle, which focuses on character development. You will take about five minutes to talk to your players and lead them in an activity that relates to one of the four core values—caring, honesty, respect, and responsibility. Following this, you'll wrap up the practice with a reminder of the next practice day and time and a preview of what you will teach in the next practice session.

A note about fitness and team circles: these times are meant to be true discussions—not lectures in which you do all the talking and the players do all the listening. Ask the questions provided and wait for your players to respond. Don't feed them the answers that we provide; we intend these answers only to help you guide the discussion. Your role is as much to ask questions and get players to respond as it is to dole out information.

The plans in this chapter, combined with the information in the rest of this book, should give you what you need to lead practices. Just remember to be patient and caring as you work on skills. Different children will progress at different rates, and it's more important that they learn the sport in a positive way than that they learn quickly.

Figures 6.1a-b and 6.2 show some simple ways to set up the field for 1 v 1 and 2 v 2 activities. Don't spend a lot of time setting up sidelines for these games. Simply encourage players to come back to their own fields if they stray.

Key to Diagrams

⊗	=	Ball
△	=	Cone
---→	=	Pass
——→	=	Run
∼∼∼→	=	Dribble
------►	=	Shot
X	=	Field player
A	=	Attacker
D	=	Defender
C	=	Coach
FD	=	Feeder
R	=	Retriever
▭	=	Small goal
- - - - -	=	Field boundaries
∧∧∧	=	Rolling the ball

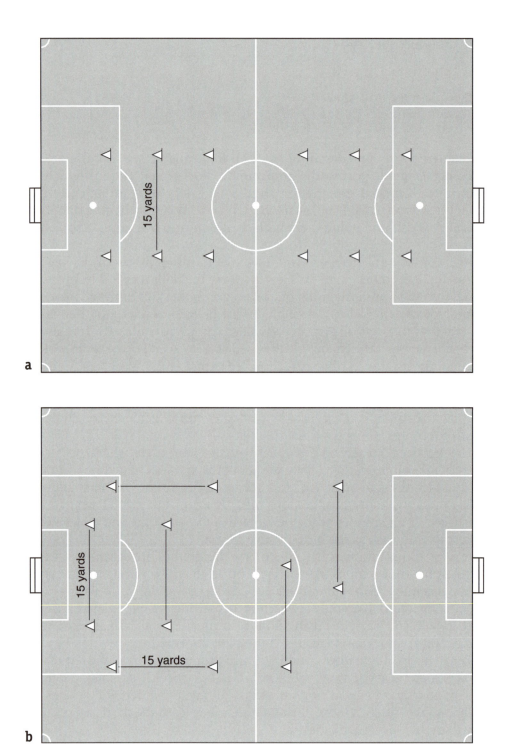

Figure 6.1 Setup for 1 v 1 activities.

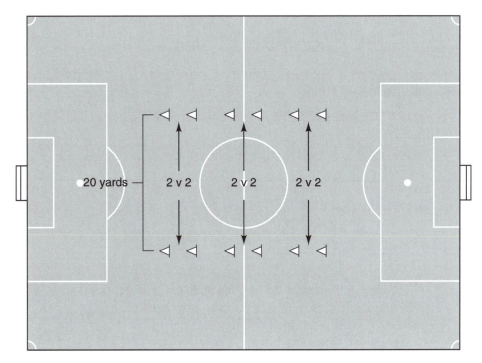

Figure 6.2 Setup for 2 v 2 activities

Practice 1

PURPOSE

To play a 3 v 3 game, focusing on boundaries and rules. The objective is for players to be able to play a 3 v 3 game of soccer in a predetermined area while adhering to simple start and restart rules.

Equipment

- ☑ One soccer ball per player (if possible)
- ☑ Two portable goals (8 feet by 4 feet) per team
- ☑ One cone (or other marker) per player (if possible)
- ☑ Different colored vests or shirts to differentiate teams

Warm-Up (10 minutes)

Begin each practice with 5 to 10 minutes of warm-up activities to get players loosened up and ready to go.

1. Players free kick or dribble in space (one ball per child), using no more than half a field.
2. Players dribble or kick at targets (cones) spread out in space.

Fitness Circle (5 minutes)

Following the warm-up, gather your players and briefly discuss the fitness concept for that practice. In this first practice your fitness topic will be more general, but in future practices you'll often discuss more specific concepts and issues such as safety, flexibility, healthy habits, and more.

Key Idea: General fitness

Gather children about 10 to 15 feet away from a goal or cone. "Everyone jump 10 times. Our muscles help us jump. When you use your muscles a long time without getting too tired, it improves your *endurance*, which means you can run longer without getting tired. Now run really fast to the goal and back." Wait for them to return. "Running strengthens your heart and lungs. Now touch your toes; try to keep your fingers down there while I count to 10. Stretching makes you flexible, like a rubber band. When we play soccer, our bodies run, kick, and move. It makes our bodies stronger and improves our fitness, which means we can run and play longer and faster. Having good physical fitness is important for soccer and for being healthy. At every practice we'll talk about fitness in our fitness circles."

38

Practice 1

Game 1 (10 minutes)

Following the fitness circle, get the kids playing a game. After letting the players play a while, interrupt the game for a time of questions and answers—with *you* asking the questions and your *players* providing the answers (about what the goal of the game was and what skills and tactics they needed to perform to succeed in the game). For many games, we provide diagrams or figures showing how to play the game. Also, we often provide coach's points for you to pass along to your players during the games.

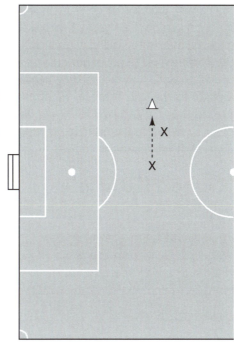

Goal

Players will learn that they have to attack a goal (cone) to score in soccer. Each team attacks a different goal (cone).

Description

1 v 1—Each player tries to hit a cone using only his or her feet, not hands. (No need for any other rules right now!)

When the question-and-answer section precedes the coach's cue, ask the questions *before* the players begin the game. Use the cue during the game.

Coach: Which way do you go when you get the ball?
Players: Toward the cone.

COACH's cue

"Go toward the cone."

☞ In games 1 and 2, watch that players don't stray too far from their cones or goals and into other games. Just redirect them if they stray. Setting up the cones for play across the field at various points will minimize the likelihood that games will spill over into each other.

In the first practice we don't include skill practices. However, after the first practice, you'll follow game 1 with a skill practice, during which you'll introduce, demonstrate, and explain a skill or tactic, then attend to your players as they practice it. The question-and-answer session, in which your players tell *you* what skills and tactics they needed to be successful in the game, leads directly to the skill practice. We often provide coach's points with the skill practices so you can pass these points along to your players. We also provide coach's cues—phrases to help your players focus on the task at hand—during many skill practices and games.

Game 2 (10 minutes)

Goal

Players will learn that they can play with others on the same team and try to score (cone or goal).

Description

2 v 2—Each pair tries to score by hitting a cone or by kicking into a small goal.

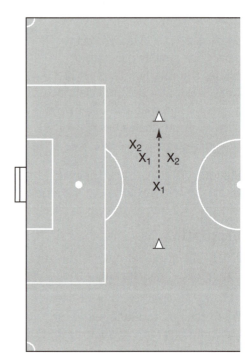

Coach: Who is on your team?
Players: (Name of teammate)

Coach: Which goal are you trying to score in?
Players: That one. (Have them point.)

Coach: Where do you kick the ball to score?
Players: In the goal. (If they say "in there," have them show you.)

COACH's cue

"Score in the goal."

40

Game 3 (20 minutes)

Goal

Players will learn appropriate ways of restarting the game when the ball goes out of play.

Description

3 v 3—Each team of three tries to score into a small goal. For each pair of teams, mark a playing area no larger than 50 by 30 feet.

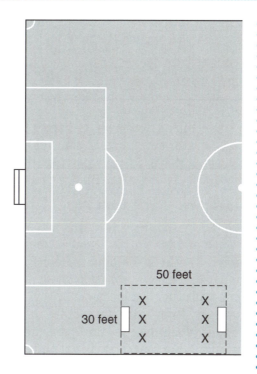

Coach: How do we start the game?
Players: With a kickoff at the center. The other team must go back into its own half.

Coach: What happens when the ball goes out-of-bounds?
Players: The other team gets to kick it in. (Don't allow throw-ins yet.)

Coach: What happens after you score a goal?
Players: A kickoff at the center. The team that scored must go back into its own half.

Team Circle
(5 minutes)

Conclude practice by gathering your players and discussing a character development concept. These aren't lectures; you want your players' active participation in these discussions. Following the discussions, wrap up the practice with a few comments.

Key Idea: Four core values

Gather children into a circle. "This season we'll talk about four qualities of a good person and teammate. Number one is *caring*. Can you tell me ways you show caring to others? Helping someone up when they fall? Good! Number two is *honesty*. What ways do you show honesty? How about if you tell someone if you played with their game or toy? That's honesty. Number three is *respect*. Do you know what respect is? One thing that shows respect is listening to adults when they speak to you, like you're doing now. Number four is *responsibility*. One way to show you're responsible is to pick up after yourself. Don't wait for others to pick up for you." Ask them to share ways they show the four values in other areas of their lives. "Good teammates show these values to each other. We'll talk more about these four values during the season."

Wrap-Up

Make summary comments about practice. Remind them of the next practice day and time, and give them a sneak preview of that practice—playing soccer with control.

Variations

Try to have enough balls and cones so that all players get plenty of touches and chances to score. This is the point of the warm-up and the 1 v 1 game. If the number of balls and cones available is limited, have players pair off and pass the ball to each other before hitting a cone.

Practice 2

Warm-Up (5 minutes)

Have players practice close dribbling. Tell players "Keep the ball close when you run," as they practice. Also, tell players that you will blow your whistle occasionally during practice. When you blow the whistle, they should stop and put a foot on the ball to show they have it under control.

Fitness Circle (5 minutes)

Key Idea: Cardiorespiratory fitness

Children gather into a group. "Everyone hold one hand up and make a fist. Squeeze your fist tightly, then let go. Keep tightening and letting go." Children continue for 10 counts. "Your heart is a special muscle that tightens and relaxes just like your fist is doing. Your heart is about the size of your fist. Let's put our fists over our chests. Every time it tightens, or beats, your heart pumps blood all over your body. When you run during soccer, your heart beats faster. The beat slows down when you slow down. Let's run with high knees for 15 counts while we count together. Stop and feel your heart beat by putting your hand over your chest." Model for players. "Running strengthens your heart and lungs and improves your fitness."

Game 1 (10 minutes)

Goal
Players will learn to control the ball.

Description
3 v 3—You review these rules with players:

- What constitutes a goal (see page 138)
- No use of hands during the game
- How to start and restart a game (see pages 135–136)

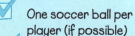
To play a 3 v 3 game, focusing on controlling the ball (as opposed to kicking it anywhere). The objective is for players to be able to move with the ball (dribble) during the 3 v 3 game.

Equipment

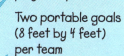

- One soccer ball per player (if possible)
- Two portable goals (8 feet by 4 feet) per team
- Different colored vests or shirts to differentiate teams

COACH's cue

"Run with the ball."

Coach: How can you get the ball up the field?
Players: Run with it.

Coach: What do we call this in soccer?
Players: Dribbling.

Coach: When you dribble the ball, should it be close to you or far away?
Players: Close to you.

Coach: What part of the foot should you use to dribble—the inside, the outside, or the toe?
Players: The inside or outside.

Skill Practice 1 (5 minutes)

1. Introduce, demonstrate, and explain how to control the ball while dribbling (see pages 124–125).
2. Practice controlling the ball while dribbling.

Description

Individual—Each player dribbles in space and changes directions when you call "turn."

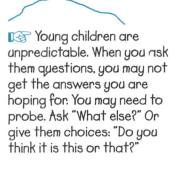

COACH's point

☞ Young children are unpredictable. When you ask them questions, you may not get the answers you are hoping for. You may need to probe. Ask "What else?" Or give them choices: "Do you think it is this or that?"

COACH's cues

"Keep the ball close."
"Use the inside and outside of both feet."
"Push the ball gently."

Skill Practice 2 (10 minutes)

1. Introduce, demonstrate, and explain how to control the ball with the inside or the outside of the foot while dribbling (see page 124).

Practice 2

2. Practice controlling the ball while dribbling with the inside or outside of the foot.

Description

Individual—First demonstrate dribbling with the inside and outside of the foot. Then have the players dribble individually while you call "turn" and "inside" or "outside" of foot.

COACH's cues

"Keep the ball close."
"Use the inside and outside of both feet."
"Push the ball gently."
"Turn inside" or "Turn outside."

Skill Practice 3 (5 minutes)

1. Introduce, demonstrate, and explain how to move the ball to avoid an opponent (see page 124-125).
2. Practice moving the ball to avoid an opponent.

Description

Individual—Each player dribbles with control to avoid an opponent, which is you. The players move freely with the ball, but must avoid you when they see you.

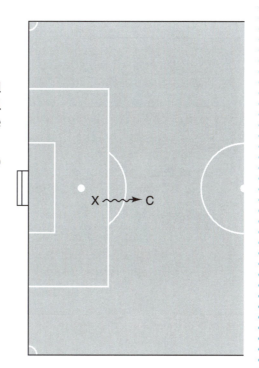

COACH's cues

"Move the ball away from me."
"Keep the ball close."
"Use the inside and outside of both feet."
"Push the ball gently."

Game 2 (15 minutes)

Goal

Players will learn to avoid opponents when they have the ball during game play.

Description

3 v 1, 3 v 2, or 3 v 3 (choose based on the skill proficiency of your players)—Players control the ball while running. Rotate players accordingly so they all have a chance to play offense and defense. (See chapter 4 for more on the use of lopsided games.)

Team Circle (5 minutes)

Key Idea: Responsibility

Gather children into a group. "I want us all to pretend we're eggs. Eggs have shells that can break. What would happen if we bumped into each other as eggs? Right. We would crack and break. Let's move around the field being eggs. Don't bump each other or we'll break!" Continue for about one minute. "We were all careful not to bump each other so our 'shells' wouldn't break! That was great! You were in charge of or 'responsible' for your moving. When we're careful of each other, we're responsible for our space and other players' space. This shows responsibility during practice and games."

Wrap-Up

Make summary comments about practice. Remind them of the next practice day and time, and give them a sneak preview of that practice—playing as a team.

Variations

A variation on skill practice 2 is to play Follow the Leader, having the players follow you and dribble as you move about the playing area at slow speed, dribbling with both feet.

Practice 3

Warm-Up (5 minutes)

1. 1 v 1—Each player tries to hit a cone using only his or her feet, not hands.
2. Players free kick or dribble in space (one ball per child), using no more than half a field.

Fitness Circle (5 minutes)

Key Idea: Muscular strength and endurance

Gather children into a circle. "Everyone find your own space so you don't bump your neighbor. You're going to run in your own spot for 30 seconds, then stop. Ready? Go!" Time children and verbally let them know the time remaining; stop them at the end of the time. "What part of the body did we just use the most when we ran?" Encourage their responses. "When we play soccer, which part of your body do you use the most?" Wait for their responses. "Muscles in our body help us move our legs. Playing soccer will help our leg muscles get stronger and grow bigger."

Game 1 (10 minutes)

Goal

Players will work with a teammate to score.

Description

2 v 2—Players kick to cones or small goals.

COACH's cue

"Help each other."

PURPOSE

To play a 3 v 3 game as a team, focusing on passing to teammates. The objective is for players to be able to advance the ball by passing to teammates.

Equipment

- ✓ One soccer ball per pair
- ✓ Two portable goals (8 feet by 4 feet) per team
- ✓ One cone per player (if possible)
- ✓ Different colored vests or shirts to differentiate teams

Coach: How can you help each other and work together to score? (You might have to prompt the answer by showing them an example. Put two players on the field, one close to the goal and the other farther back with the ball. Then ask "What is the quickest way for you two to get the ball into the goal?")
Players: Pass the ball forward toward the goal.

Skill Practice 1
(10 minutes)

1. Introduce, demonstrate, and explain how to pass accurately to a partner (see pages 125–127).

2. Practice passing accurately to a partner.

Description

Pairs—First demonstrate the proper passing technique. Then have partners practice passing, both when stationary and when moving the ball.

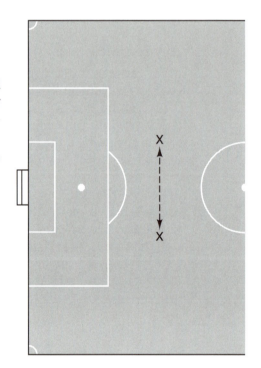

COACH's cues

"Get close to the ball."

"Face your partner."

"Turn your foot out" (so they use the inside of the foot).

"Follow through toward your partner."

Practice 3

Skill Practice 2 (10 minutes)

1. Introduce, demonstrate, and explain how to move to support a teammate with the ball (see pages 121–122).

2. Practice moving to support a teammate with the ball.

Description

Pairs—Tell partners to practice getting the ball from one end of the field to the other without running with the ball. Ask "How do you do it?" They should answer "Pass and move forward." After they practice passing the ball and score at the other end, they come back.

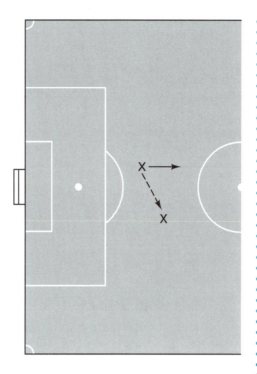

☞ Notice that some players need more attention than others with skill practice 2. Observe which pairs are struggling and provide them with a little extra help.

COACH's cue

"Pass and move ahead of your partner."

Game 2 (15 minutes)

Goal

Players will learn to pass and move ahead during the game.

Description

3 v 1, 3 v 2, or 3 v 3 (choose based on the skill proficiency of your players)—Each team of three tries to pass often during the game. Rotate players accordingly so they all have a chance to play offense and defense.

"Pass and move ahead."

Team Circle
(5 minutes)

Key Idea: Honesty

Gather children into a group near two cones about 10 feet apart. "Can you touch the ball with your hand in soccer? Even if it's an accident? Those of you who think it's okay to touch the ball, stand by this cone. Those who think it's not okay, stand by this one." Wait for children to choose. Then ask them why they chose the cone they did. "Touching the ball with your hand, even if it's an accident, is a foul. What should you do if that happens? Those of you who think you should just keep playing, stay at this cone; those of you who think you should raise your hand and give the ball to the other team, go stand by that cone." Wait for everyone to finish choosing. "It's important to be honest about fouls. If you touch the ball with your hand, even if nobody sees it, raise your hand and give the ball to the other team."

Wrap-Up

Make summary comments about practice. Remind them of the next practice day and time, and give them a sneak preview of that practice— keeping possession of the ball.

Variations

In skill practice 1, more advanced players will pick up the skill quickly. Have these players also use the outside of the foot (by turning the foot inward rather than outward).

Practice 4

Warm-Up (5 minutes)

Repeat skill practices 1 and 2 from practice 3.

Fitness Circle (5 minutes)

Key Idea: Safety equipment and rules

Bring a small piece of cardboard or a clipboard that can be used as a shield. Get one child to demonstrate. Provide a ball and have the child kick the ball at you at a medium effort. "Watch where the ball goes when Julia kicks it." Allow the ball to hit your legs. Then put the board in front of you, between you and the child kicking. Have the child kick again. "Now watch where the ball goes. This board is just like a shin guard that we wear on our legs. Wearing shin guards protects our legs just like the board protected my legs from the ball." Give each player a turn kicking the ball. "Can you think of other ways to be safe that you should remember to do when you play soccer?"

Game 1 (10 minutes)

Goal

Players will remember to move the ball downfield by passing.

Description

3 v 3—Each team of three tries to pass often during the game.

COACH's cue

"Pass and move ahead."

☞ **PURPOSE**

To keep possession of the ball, focusing on passing and receiving. The objective is for players to be able to receive the ball and dribble with it under control during game play.

Equipment

☑ One soccer ball per pair

☑ Two portable goals (8 feet by 4 feet) per team or two cones per team of three

☑ Different colored vests or shirts to differentiate teams

☑ A small piece of cardboard or a clipboard

COACH's point

☞ Emphasize and encourage passing in the game. Freeze the game when you see it happen, and point out good passing, receiving, and dribbling under control.

Coach: What do you need to do when the ball comes to you?
Players: Stop it.

Coach: How do you stop it?
Players: (Various answers, to which you could respond, "Yes, you can.")

Coach: Why don't we practice stopping the ball when it comes?

Skill Practice 1 (10 minutes)

1. Introduce, demonstrate, and explain how to receive a pass and control the ball (see page 128).
2. Practice receiving passes and controlling the ball.

Description
Groups of three—Each group passes in a triangle formation, focusing on receiving the ball.

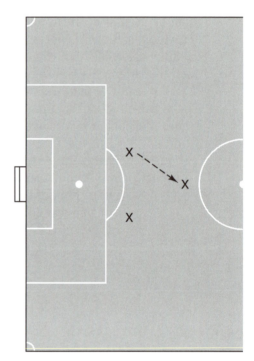

COACH's cues

"Get behind the ball."
"Use the inside or outside of the foot."
"Push the ball gently toward the player you will pass to next."
"Make the next pass."

Skill Practice 2 (10 minutes)

1. Introduce, demonstrate, and explain how to receive a pass and move with the ball under control (see page 128).
2. Practice receiving passes and moving with the ball under control.

COACH's cue

Demonstrate skills! A good picture paints a thousand words.

Description

Groups of three—In a triangle formation, each person receives the ball and dribbles a little before passing.

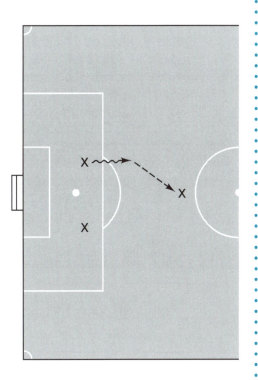

COACH's cues

"Push the ball into space."
"Dribble keeping the ball close."
"Find a teammate and pass."

Game 2 (15 minutes)

Goal

Players will learn how to receive the ball and dribble under control.

Description

3 v 1, 3 v 2, or 3 v 3 (choose based on skill proficiency of your players)—Each team of three tries to pass often during the game. Rotate players accordingly so they all have a chance to play offense and defense.

Team Circle (5 minutes)

Key Idea: Caring

Gather children into a circle. Stand in the middle of the group with a ball. Pass to each child and give him or her a turn to pass back to you. "I am going to pass the ball. If a pass comes to you, pass the ball back to me." Work around the whole circle. Talk to the children about playing and learning when they come to practice. "Who had a turn to touch the ball?" Wait for their responses. "I made sure everyone had a chance to touch the ball. Raise your hand if it felt good to be able to have a turn. How would you have felt if you did not have a turn?" Listen to their responses. "We need to share the ball and take turns so everyone can learn and play. Sharing and taking turns shows you care."

Wrap-Up

Make summary comments about practice. Remind them of the next practice day and time, and give them a sneak preview of that practice—supporting your teammates.

Variations

- Encourage better players to use both feet during practices. Also, have better players move the triangle over the field as they pass.
- Spend extra time with weaker players to help them control the ball when it comes. This is a critical skill for all players to acquire.

Practice 5

Warm-Up (5 minutes)

Repeat skill practices 1 and 2 from practice 4. Use skill practice 2 with the better players.

Fitness Circle (5 minutes)

Key Idea: Healthy habits

Gather children into a circle. "When your body doesn't eat healthy foods and get enough sleep, it moves slowly. Let's pretend we have no energy to move because we didn't eat enough healthy foods or get enough sleep." Begin to move slowly and encourage children to follow. Move extremely slowly. "Everyone stop. Now I am going to fill your bodies up with healthy foods." Act out giving them foods. "Pretend we're sleeping. When I say 'Wake up!' you can move faster because you have enough energy and enough rest. Wake up and move faster. Stop! What are some other healthy habits you have learned?" Examples: daily exercise, brushing teeth, saying no to drugs, no smoking. "It's important for everyone to practice healthy habits."

☞ PURPOSE

To keep possession of the ball by supporting teammates who have it. The objective is for players to be able to move to a good position to receive a pass when a teammate has the ball during a game.

Equipment

☑ One soccer ball per team of three

☑ Two portable goals (8 feet by 4 feet) per team or two cones per team of three

☑ Different colored vests or shirts to differentiate teams

Game 1 (10 minutes)

Goal

Players will try to help teammates. (Explain that a regulation game has 11 v 11 and that all players spread over the field so they can help or support each other.)

Description

3 v 3—Each team tries to have teammates help each other during the game.

Coach: Where can you go to help a teammate who has the ball? (You may have to show them an example. Put a defender in front of the player with the ball so that the player who wants to receive the ball has to move away into space. Then ask "If Katie has the ball here, where can Matthew go so that Katie can pass to him?")
Players: To space.

Skill Practice 1 (10 minutes)

1. Introduce, demonstrate, and explain how to stay in space to receive passes (see page 122).
2. Practice staying in space to receive passes.

Description

Teams of three, unopposed—Each team tries to make four passes as it moves to the end of the field.

COACH's cues

"Pass and move forward into space."
"Receive and pass to a teammate."

Skill Practice 2 (10 minutes)

1. Introduce, demonstrate, and explain how to create a passing lane away from the defender (see page 123).
2. Practice moving to create a passing lane away from the defender.

Description

Teams of three—You oppose each group for one or two passes, then move to the next group when it begins.

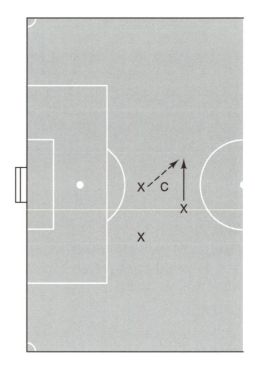

COACH's cues

"Move away from me so he (or she) can pass to you."
"Pass the ball by me."

Practice 5

Game 2 (15 minutes)

Goal

Players will learn to pass the ball effectively before shooting at the goal.

Description

3 v 1, 3 v 2, or 3 v 3 (choose based on skill proficiency of your players)—Each team tries to pass the ball three times before shooting at the goal. Rotate players accordingly so they all have a chance to play offense and defense.

Team Circle (5 minutes)

Key Idea: Caring

Gather children into a group about 10 feet from two cones that form a goal. "Let's pretend we're playing a soccer game. Watch what I do with the ball." Tell a child in the group you're passing to him. Make a bad pass. "That pass wasn't very good, was it? What would you say to me so that I don't feel bad about the pass?" As children respond, have each player who makes a supportive comment take an open shot on goal. If players make nonsupportive comments, encourage them to change their words to become more supportive; after they have changed the words, have each of them take an open shot at the goal. "It's very important to support your teammates, especially when they make mistakes. Saying something that makes someone feel good shows you care."

Wrap-Up

Make summary comments about practice. Remind them of the next practice day and time, and give them a sneak preview of that practice—keep-away games.

COACH's point

☞ Freeze game 2 occasionally to show players where good supporting positions are. Watch that players don't try to support by getting too close to teammates who have the ball. This only makes the game more crowded, so encourage them to stay in space to receive a pass.

Variations

- Encourage better players to use both feet.
- Make better players work harder to get the ball around you in skill practice 2.

Practice 6

☞ PURPOSE

To keep possession of the ball in a game, focusing on passing, receiving, and supporting under pressure. The objective is for players to be able to keep possession of the ball in the 3 v 3 game by passing well, receiving the ball effectively, and supporting teammates who have the ball.

Equipment

☑ One soccer ball per team of three

☑ Two portable goals (8 feet by 4 feet) per team or two cones per team of three

☑ Different colored vests or shirts to differentiate teams

☑ A rubber band

Warm-Up (5 minutes)

Repeat skill practice 2 from practice 4.

Fitness Circle (5 minutes)

Key Idea: Flexibility

Bring a rubber band to use as a prop. "This rubber band is like our muscles. When I pull it, it stretches; when I let go, it pulls back to its original shape." Demonstrate with the rubber band, stretching it out and back, using a gentle, slow action. "Your muscles work the same way. When you reach and stretch, your muscles are stretching just like the rubber band. When your body comes back, your muscles go back to their original shape. Everyone reach down to the ground with your arms slowly, and then bring your arms back up." Have children repeat three times. "Your leg muscles need to stretch because you use them the most in soccer; stretching makes your leg muscles more flexible. When muscles are flexible, it keeps them from getting hurt and makes the muscles feel good."

Game 1 (10 minutes)

Goal

Players will learn to keep the ball away from the other team and score.

Description

3 v 3—Each team tries to pass three times before scoring a goal. If they do, give them an extra point for that goal.

Coach: How can you keep the ball as a team?
Players: Pass.

Coach: What do you need to do as well as passing?
Players: Receive and control.

Coach: If a player with the ball wants to pass, what does he or she need? (Again, you may need to set this up in a demonstration.)
Players: Someone to pass to.

Practice 6

Skill Practice 1
(10 minutes)

1. Introduce, demonstrate, and explain how to create a passing lane around a defender (see page 122).

2. Practice moving to create a passing lane around a defender.

Description

Groups of three—Each team tries to pass in a triangle formation, with you opposing.

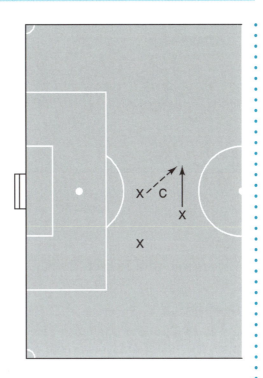

COACH's cues

"Move to help your teammate."
"Pass and control the ball."

Skill Practice 2
(10 minutes)

1. Introduce, demonstrate, and explain how to support a teammate under pressure (see page 122).

2. Practice supporting a teammate under pressure.

Description

2 v 1—Players practice in an area 20 feet by 10 feet with a small goal. The two attackers must pass three times before scoring in the goal while defended by the third player.

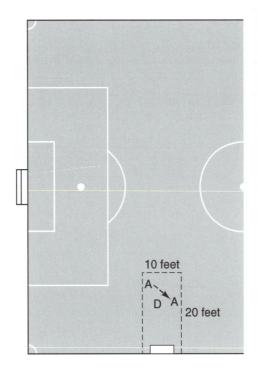

COACH's point

☞ Remember to have the players rotate playing the defender in skill practice 2. If necessary, guide players to the right answers as you ask questions by setting up scenarios (e.g., if Katie wants to pass to Michael or Kolicia, where do they have to be?).

59

COACH's cue

"Pass and move quickly."

Game 2 (15 minutes)

Goal

Players will learn to keep the ball by good passing, control, and support.

Description

3 v 1, 3 v 2, or 3 v 3 (choose based on the skill proficiency of your players)—Rotate players accordingly so they all have a chance to play offense and defense.

COACH's cues

"Pass and support."
"Move forward."
"Control the ball."

Team Circle
(5 minutes)

Key Idea: Responsibility

Gather children into a circle. You're in the middle of the circle with a ball. You'll try to kick the ball out of the circle. The children will have two chances to keep the ball from escaping the circle. During one turn they'll use minimal effort, and during the second they'll use their maximum effort. "I am going to try to kick the ball out of the circle. Everyone work together to keep the ball in the circle. Pretend that you are snails that can't get to the ball fast enough." Begin to dribble and try to get the ball out of the circle, reminding players that snails move slowly. "This time move like busy bees that fly fast and keep moving." Repeat activity, encouraging players to be "busy bees." "When you try to be like busy bees, you're being responsible to your teammates."

Wrap-Up

Make summary comments about practice. Remind them of the next practice day and time, and give them a sneak preview of that practice—shooting at the goal.

Variations

Apply more pressure to better players during practice 1. This will challenge their control.

Practice 1

PURPOSE

To attack the goal, focusing on shooting a stationary and moving ball. The objective is for players to be able to shoot a stationary or moving ball accurately at the goal during practice and game play.

Equipment

- ☑ One soccer ball per pair
- ☑ Two portable goals (8 feet by 4 feet) per team or two cones per team of three
- ☑ Different colored vests or shirts to differentiate teams

Warm-Up (10 minutes)

Groups of three—Players play 2 v 1 in an area 20 feet by 10 feet with a small goal. They must pass three times, then shoot into the goal.

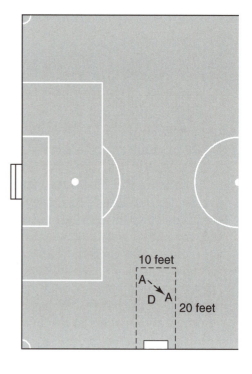

10 feet

20 feet

Fitness Circle (5 minutes)

Key Idea: Muscular strength and endurance

Gather children into a group. Show children the differences between a kick with minimal effort and one with close to maximum effort. "Watch how far the ball goes when I kick it two different times." Show both kicks to children. "Let's make a circle, and you show me how you would kick the ball. Pretend you're kicking a ball, and show me a short kick. Now step back two big steps and show me a long kick that will make the ball go across the circle." Highlight the ball going farther in the second kick. "You can kick the ball farther when your muscles in your legs are strong. Your muscles in your legs get stronger when you practice kicking."

Practice 7

Game 1 (10 minutes)

Goal

Players will learn to attempt shots at the goal.

Description

3 v 3—Players try to score as many goals as they can.

Coach: What do you have to do to score?
Players: Shoot.

Coach: When you shoot, where should you aim the ball?
Players: At the goal.

Skill Practice 1 (10 minutes)

1. Introduce, demonstrate, and explain how to accurately shoot a stationary ball into the goal (see page 129).

2. Practice accurately shooting a stationary ball into the goal without pressure.

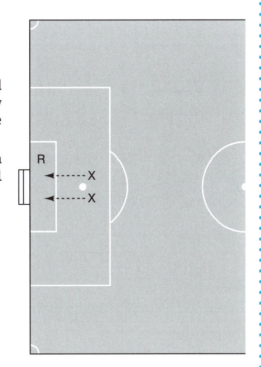

Description

Groups of three—Have one retriever and two shooters. Each shooter shoots a stationary ball into the goal he or she is attacking.

COACH's cues

"Get close to the ball." (Use a long stride to plant the nonstriking foot beside the ball.)
"Use the laces to kick the ball."
"Keep the toe down as you shoot."

Skill Practice 2 (10 minutes)

1. Introduce, demonstrate, and explain how to accurately shoot a moving ball into the goal (see page 129).
2. Practice accurately shooting a moving ball into the goal.

Description

Groups of three—You or one of the teammates rolls the ball forward so the shooters can move in and shoot the moving ball.

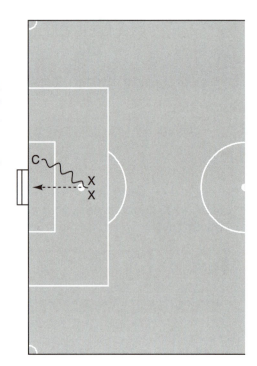

COACH's cues

"Catch up to the ball."
"Shoot before the ball stops rolling."
"Get close to the ball, use laces, toe down."

Game 2 (10 minutes)

Goal

Players will learn to shoot accurately in the game.

Description

3 v 1, 3 v 2, or 3 v 3 (choose based on the skill proficiency of your players)—Emphasize shooting to score. Rotate players accordingly so they all have a chance to play offense and defense.

COACH's point

☞ Have teams count the number of goals they score in game 1, and see if they can score more in game 2. This way they see the value of practice.

Practice 7

Team Circle
(5 minutes)

Key Idea: Respect

Gather children into a group. "I'm going to ask you some questions about things I notice on this team. Tell me if you agree. Do you try to learn new skills at practice? Do you work hard to improve your skills? Do you help your teammates? Do you follow directions? Do you feel good about yourselves when you play a good game?" Listen to responses following each question. "Think about players who will be your opponents. What qualities or things do they have or do? Are they the same as you?" Listen for "yes" or "no." "It's important to think of our opponents in the same way we think of ourselves. You respect yourself, and you should respect your opponents. They are a lot like you and are learning the same things."

Wrap-Up

Make summary comments about practice. Remind them of the next practice day and time, and give them a sneak preview of that practice—shooting under pressure.

Variations

Have better players shoot from farther away during the practices.

Practice 8

PURPOSE

To attack the goal, focusing on shooting a moving ball under pressure. The objective is for players to be able to shoot under pressure from a defender during game play.

Equipment

- ☑ One soccer ball per pair
- ☑ Two portable goals (8 feet by 4 feet) per team or two cones per team of three
- ☑ Different colored vests or shirts to differentiate teams

Warm-Up (10 minutes)

Players shoot a stationary ball into a goal.

Fitness Circle (5 minutes)

Key Idea: Training and conditioning

Gather children into a circle. "What will you do tonight after you eat dinner?" Wait for their responses. "At the end of the day, what do you do?" Encourage children to discuss sleep. "Let's pretend you are at your homes, and you climb into bed to go to sleep. Everyone lie down. Now let's pretend it's morning and a new day. You don't have soccer practice today. Your body needs to move every day to stay in good physical condition for soccer. What should we do to move our bodies?" Wait for their responses. If a child suggests an activity (e.g., biking, walking, swimming), have everyone pretend to do that activity. Then have them "sleep" again, wake up, and choose another physical activity idea.

Game 1 (10 minutes)

Goal

Players will learn to shoot often.

Description

3 v 3, shooting to goals

COACH's cue

"Shoot when you have a chance."

Practice 8

Coach: Do you always have a lot of time to shoot in a game?
Players: No, sometimes you have to hurry.

Coach: When do you have to hurry?
Players: When an opponent is close to you.

Skill Practice (15 minutes)

1. Introduce, demonstrate, and explain how to shoot accurately under pressure (see page 129).
2. Practice shooting accurately under pressure from a defender.

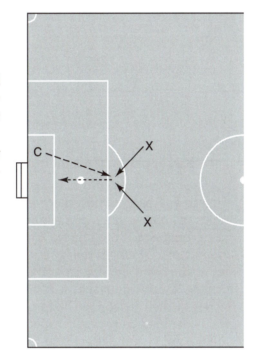

Description

Pairs of players—You feed the ball between two players who chase it toward the goal. The first player to reach the ball must shoot as quickly as possible. This teaches shooting under pressure.

COACH's cues

"Chase hard."
"Shoot quickly."

COACH's point

☞ For the skill practice, the best place to start feeding the ball is from the middle of the field. When one of the first pair has scored, the pair returns to the starting point by coming back down the sides of the field while you feed the next pair. As it takes players some time to return to the starting point, this practice might involve several pairs.

Game 2 (15 minutes)

Goals

Players will learn to attempt more shots and shoot accurately under pressure during game play.

Description

3 v 1, 3 v 2, or 3 v 3 (choose based on the skill proficiency of your players)—Rotate players accordingly so they all have a chance to play offense and defense.

COACH's cue

"Shoot quickly when you get the chance."

Team Circle (5 minutes)

Key Idea: Responsibility

Gather children into a group. Dump five to six balls out of a mesh ball bag, leaving them where they stop. "Pretend we just finished one activity in practice and we're getting ready to do something else. Everyone walk away from the balls and make a group circle." Pick up the balls, then go to the group. Dump balls out again. "Now come back and you pick up the balls, then go make a circle. Which way makes it faster for me to get to your circle?" Listen to their responses. "What do you think we should do with the balls?" Listen to their responses. Discuss picking up equipment before doing another activity. "We can have more fun and learn more when we work together. That is a shared responsibility between the coach and the players."

Wrap-Up

Make summary comments about practice. Remind them of the next practice day and time, and give them a sneak preview of that practice—guarding or marking your opponents.

Variations

- Keep the feeds simple for weaker players. A low, rolling ball is easy to control and shoot.
- Vary the feeds for better players so the ball bounces a little, making control before the shot more challenging.

Practice 9

Warm-Up (10 minutes)

1 v 1—Each player tries to hit a cone using only his or her feet, not hands.

Fitness Circle (5 minutes)

Key Idea: Muscular strength and endurance

Have children spread out in a group. "Put your hand on the front of your thigh, then lift it up and set it down. Did you feel the muscle get tight when you lifted it up and then relax when you set it down? Try it again five times." Assist players if needed. "Muscles tighten, or contract, when you move. You use the thigh muscles, or quadriceps, when you kick the ball in soccer. The more you practice kicking the stronger your thigh, or quadriceps muscles, will get; that's called improving your muscular strength."

Game 1 (10 minutes)

Goal

Players will learn to stop the other team from getting the ball.

Description

3 v 3, shooting to goals

Coach: How can you stop players on the other team from getting the ball?
Players: Stand close to them.

Coach: If I want to pass to Katie, where can Matthew go to make it hard for Katie and me?
Players: Next to Katie.

☞ **PURPOSE**

To defend space, focusing on marking (guarding) opponents. The objective is for players to be able to defend space in a game by marking opposing players.

Equipment

☑ One soccer ball per pair

☑ Two portable goals (8 feet by 4 feet) per team

☑ One cone (or other marker) per player (if possible)

☑ Different colored vests or shirts to differentiate teams

Skill Practice 1 (5 minutes)

1. Introduce, demonstrate, and explain how to follow an opponent (see page 130).
2. Practice following an opponent.

Description

Pairs—When you call "go," one player tries to get away from the other. When you call "stop," the players switch roles, then repeat.

COACH's cues

"Watch your opponent."
"Stay close to him or her."

Skill Practice 2 (15 minutes)

1. Introduce, demonstrate, and explain how to mark an opponent who is trying to receive a pass (see page 130).
2. Practice marking an opponent who is trying to get free to receive a pass.

Description

Groups of three—One player feeds the ball to the attacker. The attacker tries to get free from the defender. Play stops when the attacker or the defender has the ball in space; they then do it again.

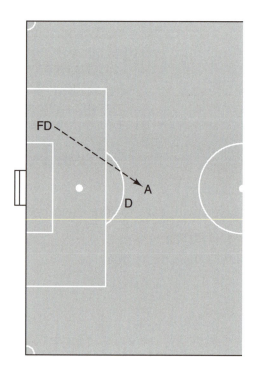

COACH's cue

"Mark your opponent."

COACH's point

☞ In skill practice 2, you may need to take over as feeder, depending on the ability of the third player to feed accurately. Rotate the third player into the practice every two or three trials.

Practice 9

Game 2 (10 minutes)

Goal

Players will learn to mark effectively when on defense in the game.

Description

3 v 3

COACH's cue

"Mark an opponent when the other team has the ball."

COACH's point

☞ Freeze game 2 occasionally to check on whether players know who they should be marking.

Team Circle (5 minutes)

Key Idea: Respect

Gather children into a single-file line near two cones about 10 feet apart. "I am going to walk down the line two times. Remember how it feels each time I pass you." Walk down the line and nod to each player. Repeat, but this time tell each player "great game" or "nice play today" and shake his or her hand. "Which time that I passed you made you feel better?" Ask children to stand near a cone that represents their choice. "Shaking hands and saying 'good game' are important traditions that show we appreciate our opponents' efforts in a game. It shows respect for your opponents." Divide team in half and have them practice an end-of-game "respect ritual."

Wrap-Up

Make summary comments about practice. Remind them of the next practice day and time, and give them a sneak preview of that practice—challenging your opponent for the ball.

Variations

Use a ball in practice 1. Player A can try to get away from player B while dribbling a ball.

71

Practice 10

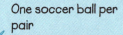

PURPOSE

To defend your own space in a game, focusing on pressuring the ball. The objective is for players to be able to pressure opponents who have the ball during game play.

Equipment

- ☑ One soccer ball per pair
- ☑ Two portable goals (8 feet by 4 feet) per team
- ☑ One cone (or other marker) per player (if possible)
- ☑ Different colored vests or shirts to differentiate teams

Warm-Up (10 minutes)

1 v 1—Each player tries to hit a cone or small goal using only his or her feet, not hands.

Fitness Circle (5 minutes)

Key Idea: Healthy habits

Gather children into a group. Mark boundary areas. "When I say, 'go!' you are all going to run as fast as you can, without bumping each other, staying in this area. Ready, go!" Children run for about a minute or until they get tired. "You had enough energy to run. But when you don't take care of your body, you can get tired much faster playing soccer. I am going to say a habit, and you shout if it's healthy or unhealthy." (Examples: taking drugs, smoking, brushing teeth, drinking plenty of water, getting plenty of sleep and rest, eating a variety of foods.) "Can you think of any others? Healthy or unhealthy?"

Game 1 (10 minutes)

Goal

Players will learn to watch an opponent and stay close.

Description

3 v 3—Each team tries to stop the other team from scoring.

Coach: If the opponent you are marking gets the ball, where should you move?
Players: Closer to him or her.

Coach: As the opponent you are marking gets closer to your goal, where should you move?
Players: Closer to him or her.

Coach: How should you move (quickly or slowly)?
Players: Quickly.

Practice 10

Skill Practice (15 minutes)

1. Introduce, demonstrate, and explain how to pressure an opponent in possession of the ball (see page 130).

2. Practice pressuring an opponent who is in possession of the ball.

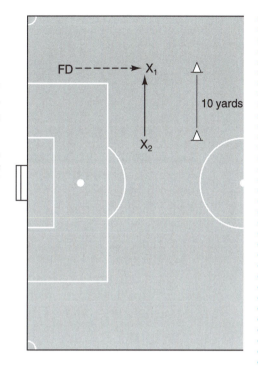

Description

Groups of three—Set the cones about 10 yards apart. Players 1 and 2 each have a cone, and each stands by the cone to start. A feeder feeds the ball to player 1. Player 2 closes the gap as quickly as possible, trying to prevent player 1 from dribbling to player 2's cone. Rotate the feeder into the practice every two trials.

"Go to the player with the ball."
"Move quickly."

Game 2 (15 minutes)

Goal

Players will learn to mark tightly and pressure the ball carrier during game play.

Description

3 v 3

☞ Freeze the game from time to time to show good marking and to check that players are marking appropriately.

Team Circle
(5 minutes)

Key Idea: Keeping perspective

Gather children into a group near two cones about 10 feet apart. "What did you most enjoy learning about in soccer this season?" Listen to their responses. "Players who thought they tried their best to learn, stand by this cone. Players who think they had fun this season, stand by this one. Both of those are important. You should try your best and have fun no matter what happens during the season. The most important thing in soccer is to have fun playing with friends and to learn new skills. I think you all did that! Next year is another chance to have fun and make new friends!"

Wrap-Up

Make summary comments about what everyone learned over the season. Encourage players to come back next year!

Variations

In the skill practice, vary the distance apart that players start. High-ability players can start farther apart, giving the defender more distance to cover to close down the space.

Practice Plans for Six- to Seven-Year-Olds

This chapter presents 10 practice plans you'll use with your six- to seven-year-old YMCA Rookies team. The plans are based on a 4 v 4 game, again with simple rules for scoring and starting and restarting the game. The field should be approximately 40 yards long and 30 yards wide, with a goal about 4 feet high and 8 feet wide, without a goalkeeper. Use a size 3 ball.

At this level, we further develop rules for restarting to resemble the real game, and having four players on each team enables participants to experience situations of game complexity. The game still provides each child with many opportunities to play the ball without undue pressure and reinforces the concept of playing within a boundary, thereby forcing players to try to control the ball.

Each plan contains the following sections:

- ◎ Purpose
- ◎ Equipment
- ◎ Practice Plan
- ◎ Coach's Points
- ◎ Variations

Purpose focuses on what you want to teach your players during that practice; it is your main theme for the day. *Equipment* notes what you'll need on hand for that practice. We'll address *practice plan* in depth in just a moment. *Coach's points* are helpful reminders for you, points of emphasis to most effectively conduct the practice. Finally, *variations* provide ideas for making the game more or less difficult, to match the abilities of your players. We include variations to games at the end of each plan, providing you with modifications to keep skill practices and games fun and interesting and to help players of varying skill levels.

The practice plan section outlines what you will do during each practice session. It consists of these elements:

◎ Warm-Up

◎ Fitness Circle

◎ Game 1

◎ Skill Practices or Games

◎ Team Circle and Wrap-Up

You'll begin each session with 5- to 10-minute warm-up activities. (*Note:* All times given in the practice plans are approximate.) Follow this with 5 minutes of the fitness circle, during which you briefly talk with players and lead them in an activity that relates to health or fitness. Then, in game 1, you'll be working on the first two steps of the four-step process for teaching soccer: playing a modified soccer game and helping them discover what they need to do. We designed the game to focus players' attention on a particular aspect of soccer. Start the game but, when it's clear that the players are having trouble achieving the goal of the game, stop the game and ask questions and get answers similar to those shown in the plans. The questions and answers will help the players see what skills they need to solve tactical problems in the game. (Occasionally, when the question-and-answer section precedes the coach's cue, ask the questions *before* the players begin the game and use the cue during the game.)

The third part of the four-step process is teaching the skills identified in game 1 through the skill practices. In each skill practice you'll use the IDEA approach to

◎ introduce the skill;

◎ demonstrate the skill;

◎ explain the skill; and

◎ attend to players practicing the skill.

Chapter 8 contains descriptions of all the skills, so we will give a page reference to guide you to the appropriate description. The introduction, demonstration, and explanation should be brief, to fit young children's short attention spans. Then, as the players practice, you will attend to individual children and guide them with coach's cues or further demonstration.

After the skill practices, you will finish the four-step process by having the children play another game. This let's them use the skills they just learned and develop their understanding of how to use those skills in the context of a game. Note that in game 1, when players are being introduced to a new tactic or skill, they usually will play an even-sided game (such as 3 v 3). This allows them to encounter the challenges they will face in executing the tactic or skill. Then, in most game 2s, they play lopsided games (such as 3 v 1 or 3 v 2) to increase their chances of experiencing success and beginning to master the new tactic or skill. However, if your players are showing proficiency with the new tactic or skill, you can use even-sided games in game 2. The choice is yours; for more on this issue, see chapter 4.

The practice plan section concludes with a team circle, which focuses on character development. You will take about five minutes to talk to your players and lead them in an activity that relates to one of the four core values—caring, honesty, respect, and responsibility. Following this, you'll wrap up the practice with a reminder of the next practice day and time and a preview of what you will teach in the next practice session.

A note about fitness and team circles: these times are meant to be true discussions—not lectures in which you do all the talking and the players do all the listening. Ask the questions provided and wait for your players to respond. Don't feed them the answers that we provide; we intend these answers only to help you guide the discussion. Your role is as much to ask questions and get players to respond as it is to dole out information.

The plans in this chapter, combined with the information in the rest of this book, should give you what you need to lead practices. Just remember to be patient and caring as you work on skills. Different children will progress at different rates, and it's more important that they learn the sport in a positive way than that they learn quickly.

Key to Diagrams

⊗	=	Ball
△	=	Cone
- - - ➤	=	Pass
⟶	=	Run
∿➤	=	Dribble
------➤	=	Shot
X	=	Field player
A	=	Attacker
D	=	Defender
C	=	Coach
FD	=	Feeder
R	=	Retriever
▭	=	Small goal
- - - - -	=	Field boundaries
∧∧∧	=	Rolling the ball

Practice 1

PURPOSE

To play the 4 v 4 game, focusing on boundaries and rules. Players will be able to play a 4 v 4 game of soccer in a predetermined area while adhering to simple start and restart rules.

Equipment

- ☑ One soccer ball per player (if possible)
- ☑ Two portable goals (8 feet by 4 feet) or two pairs of cones per eight players
- ☑ One cone (or other marker) per player (if possible)
- ☑ Different colored vests or shirts to differentiate teams

Warm-Up (10 minutes)

Begin each practice with 5 to 10 minutes of warm-up activities to get players loosened up and ready to go.

1. Players kick or dribble in space (one ball per child).
2. Players dribble or kick at targets spread out in space.

Fitness Circle (5 minutes)

Following the warm-up, gather your players and briefly discuss the fitness concept for that practice.

Key Idea: General fitness

Gather players into a group. "In soccer, running makes our hearts beat faster, and kicking helps strengthen our leg muscles so we can kick the ball farther. Spread out into your own space. Everyone run in place and I will pass the ball to some of you. If you get the ball, pass it back to me and keep running!" Continue for about 30 seconds. "Playing soccer improves our physical conditioning or fitness. We get better at running and kicking the ball, and can keep going longer before we get too tired. How can I keep from getting too tired when I'm running?" (Pacing themselves.) "How about kicking?" (Practicing at home.) "It's also important to take a rest when you need one and to drink water during practice and at home. We'll talk more about the different areas of fitness in our fitness circles throughout the season."

Game 1 (10 minutes)

Following the fitness circle, get the kids playing a game. After letting the players play for a while, interrupt the game for a time of questions and answers—with *you* asking the questions and your *players* providing the answers (about what the goal of the game was and what skills and tactics they needed to perform to succeed in the game). For many games, we provide diagrams or figures showing how to play the game. Also, we often provide coach's points for you to pass along to your players during the games.

Goal

Players will learn that they have to attack a goal (cone) to score in soccer. Each team attacks a different goal.

Practice 1

Description

1 v 1—Each player tries to hit a cone using only his or her feet, not hands. (No need for any other rules right now!)

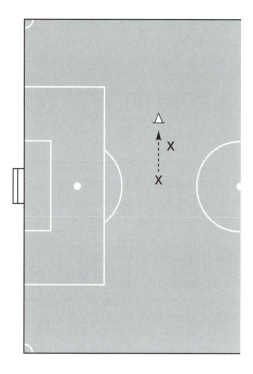

When the question-and-answer section precedes the coach's cues, ask the questions before the players begin the game. Use the cues during the game.

Coach: Which way do you go when you get the ball?
Players: Toward the cone.

"Go toward the cone."

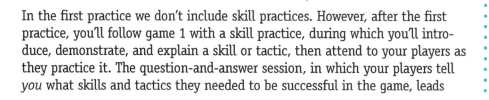

In the first practice we don't include skill practices. However, after the first practice, you'll follow game 1 with a skill practice, during which you'll introduce, demonstrate, and explain a skill or tactic, then attend to your players as they practice it. The question-and-answer session, in which your players tell *you* what skills and tactics they needed to be successful in the game, leads directly to the skill practice. We often provide coach's points with the skill practices for you to pass along to your players. We also provide coach's cues— phrases to help your players focus on the task at hand—during many skill practices and games.

Game 2 (10 minutes)

Goal

Players will learn that they can play with other players on the same team and try to score between the posts (cones or goal).

Description

2 v 2—Each pair tries to score by hitting a cone or by kicking into a small goal.

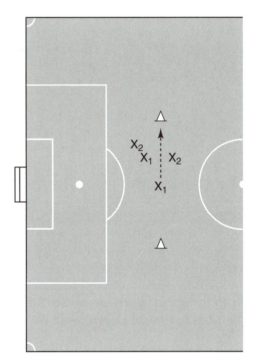

Coach: Who is on your team?
Players: (Name of teammate)

Coach: Which goal are you trying to score in?
Players: That one. (Have them point.)

Coach: Where do you kick the ball to score?
Players: In the goal. (If they say "in there," have them show you.)

COACH's point

☞ In games 1 and 2, watch that players don't stray too far from their cones or goals and into other games. Just redirect them if they stray. Setting up the cones for play across the field at various points will minimize the likelihood that games will spill over into each other.

COACH's cue

"Score in the goal."

Practice 1

Game 3 (20 minutes)

Goal

Players will learn appropriate ways of restarting the game when the ball goes out of play.

Description

4 v 4—Each team of four tries to score into a small goal. For each pair of teams, mark a playing area no larger than 50 by 30 feet.

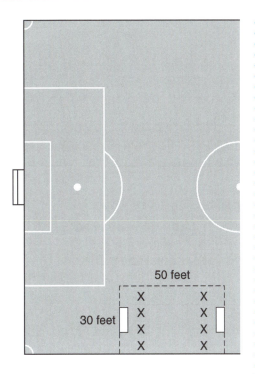

50 feet

30 feet

Coach: How do we start the game?
Players: With a kickoff at the center. The other team must go back into its own half.

Coach: What happens when the ball goes out-of-bounds at the side?
Players: It is a throw-in.*

Coach: What happens when the ball goes out-of-bounds at the end?
Players: It is a goal kick or a corner kick.**

Coach: What happens after a goal is scored?
Players: A kickoff at the center. The team that scored must go back into its own half.

COACH's cues

"Have both feet behind the line."
"Hold the ball back overhead with two hands."
"Throw to your teammate, keeping both feet on the ground."

---

* It might be worth stopping the game for five minutes so all players can practice taking throw-ins (see page 136). You can do this quickly by having pairs of players do throw-ins to each other (one ball per pair).

** You can set up and practice goal kicks and corner kicks (see pages 135–136) during the game.

Team Circle (5 minutes)

Conclude practice by gathering your players and discussing a character development concept. These aren't lectures; you want your players' active participation in these discussions. Following the discussions, wrap up the practice with a few comments.

Key Idea: Four core values

Gather children into a circle with one ball. "Everyone hand the ball to the one next to you until it makes it around the whole circle." After the ball has gone around the circle one time, have it passed to you. "We play soccer to be more healthy and fit, but it also teaches us to become good teammates and good people. This season we will talk about four qualities of a good person and teammate: *caring, honesty, respect,* and *responsibility.* Our team needs to have all of these qualities in our practices and games. Remember that we can't be a team without each of you doing your part. Let's pass the ball to each other and say one of the core values before you pass. This will help you remember to use all four of the qualities so we can work together."

Wrap-Up

Make summary comments about practice. Remind them of the next practice day and time, and give them a sneak preview of that practice: playing as a team.

Variations

• Have enough balls and cones so all players get plenty of touches and chances to score. This is the point of the warm-up and the 1 v 1 game. If the number of balls and cones available is limited, have players pair off and pass the ball to each other before hitting a cone.

• As always, you cannot be certain how many players will show up for each session, so you may not always have an even number of players for 2 v 2 or 4 v 4. To use extra players in games, you can place one player as a permanent attacker, always playing for whichever team has the ball. That way 2 v 2 becomes 2 v 2 + 1.

Practice 2

Warm-Up (5 minutes)

Have pairs of players pass and move in a small area. Tell them to call for the ball from their partners.

Fitness Circle (5 minutes)

Key Idea: Flexibility

Bring a rubber band and show it to children. "This rubber band is like our muscles. Can you tell me why?" Listen for children's responses (stretches when pulled, goes back to original shape, etc.). Demonstrate how the rubber band stretches. "Your muscles work the same way as this rubber band. When you reach and stretch, your muscles stretch just like the rubber band. When your body comes back, your muscles go back to their original shape. Everyone reach down to the ground with your arms slowly and then bring your arms back up." Have children repeat three times. "Your leg muscles need to stretch because we use them the most in soccer. It makes them more flexible. When muscles are flexible, it keeps them from getting hurt and makes the muscles feel good."

☞ **PURPOSE**

To play the 4 v 4 game as a team, focusing on positional and support play. Players will be able to effectively support teammates who have the ball in a 4 v 4 game of soccer.

Equipment

☑ One soccer ball per pair

☑ Two portable goals (8 feet by 4 feet) or two pairs of cones per eight players

☑ Different colored vests or shirts to differentiate teams

☑ A rubber band

Game 1 (10 minutes)

Goals

Players will learn to spread out down the field so they can receive a pass.

Description

4 v 4—Review the rules, including starts and restarts, fouls, no use of hands, throw-ins, corner kicks (direct only), and goal kicks (see chapter 9). Encourage players to spread out.

"Be in a space where someone can pass to you."

Coach: What is the fastest way to get the ball down the field (pass or dribble)?
Players: Pass.

Coach: For Katie to pass down the field, where does Matthew need to go so she can pass to him?
Players: Down the field.

☞ Remember that when you ask young children questions you may not get the answers you are hoping for. Young children are unpredictable. You may need to probe by asking "What else?" or to get to an answer by offering them a forced choice ("Do you think it is this or that?").

Skill Practice 1 (10 minutes)

1. Introduce, demonstrate, and explain how to move forward to support teammates (see pages 121–122).
2. Practice moving forward to support teammates.

Description

Pairs—Each pair passes the ball and moves up and down the field.

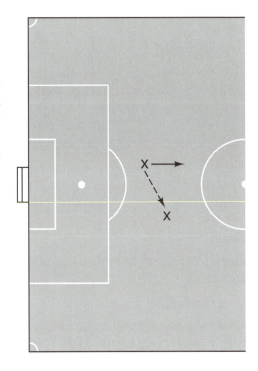

"Move downfield (toward the goal) to support your teammate."

Practice 2

Skill Practice 2 (10 minutes)

1. Introduce, demonstrate, and explain how to spread out as a team to move the ball downfield (see pages 123–124).
2. Practice spreading out as a team to move the ball downfield.

Description

Groups of four—Each group passes the ball and moves up and down the field. The object is to get the ball down the field as quickly as possible. Each player must receive at least one pass.

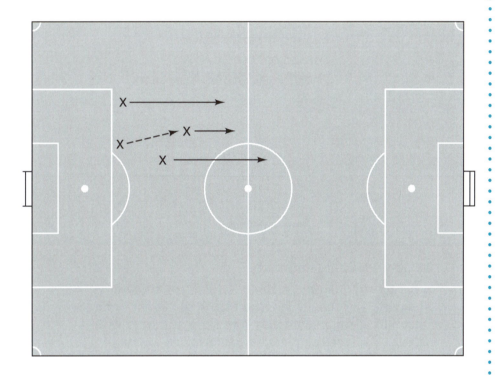

COACH's cue

"Spread out forward and sideways."

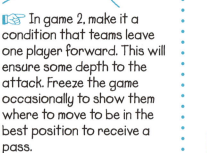

☞ In game 2, make it a condition that teams leave one player forward. This will ensure some depth to the attack. Freeze the game occasionally to show them where to move to be in the best position to receive a pass.

Game 2 (15 minutes)

Goal

Players will learn to spread out the length and width of the field.

Description

4 v 4—Each team leaves one player forward.

COACH's cues

"Leave one player forward."

"Spread out over the field."

"Look for teammates to pass to."

Team Circle (5 minutes)

Key Idea: Responsibility

Gather children into a group. "When you come to practice, you should do three things: (1) Be ready to play. (2) Learn and improve your skills and work with others. (3) Have fun. I'm going to give you a way to remember these three things. It's called a 'team motto.' Our team motto is *Play hard, play fair, and have fun!* Let's say it together loudly. That's great. Be sure to remember our team motto and put it into practice."

Wrap-Up

Make summary comments about practice. Remind them of the next practice day and time, and give them a sneak preview of that practice—supporting your teammates.

Variations

In skill practice 2, provide some light opposition for the better teams, so they must get the ball past you before getting to the other end of the field.

Practice 3

Warm-Up (5 minutes)

Players pair up. Each player has a cone, and each pair has a ball. The cones are about 10 yards apart. Each player tries to hit the opponent's cone with the ball.

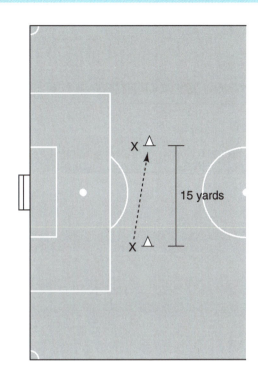

15 yards

☞ **PURP...**

To keep possession of the ball, focusing on passing in the game. The object is for players to be able to pass the ball under pressure during the 4 v 4 game.

Equipment

☑ One soccer ball per pair

☑ Two portable goals (8 feet by 4 feet) or two pairs of cones per eight players

☑ One cone (or other marker) per player (if possible)

☑ Different colored vests or shirts to differentiate teams

Fitness Circle (5 minutes)

Key Idea: Cardiorespiratory fitness

Children gather in a group. "Everyone hold one hand up and make a fist. Squeeze your fist tightly, then let go. Keep tightening and letting go." Children continue for 10 counts. "Your heart is a special muscle that tightens and relaxes just like your fist is doing. Your heart is about the size of your fist. Every time it tightens, or beats, it pumps blood all over your body. When you play soccer, your heart beats faster and you breathe faster. Run in place with high knees. Feel your lungs and feel your heart beating by placing your hands over your chest. Count how many times your heart beats." Time for 15 seconds. Ask players the number they counted. "Running helps you improve your cardiorespiratory fitness—the heart and lungs working together to get blood to your whole body."

Game 1 (10 minutes)

Goal

Players will learn to pass in the game.

Description

2 v 2 to cones or small goals—Place the cones or goals about 20 yards apart.

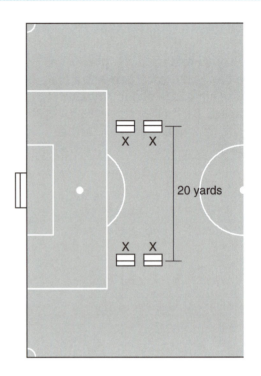

20 yards

COACH's cue

"Play as a team."

Coach: How can you best play as a team?
Players: Pass the ball to each other.

Practice 3

Skill Practice 1 (15 minutes)

1. Introduce, demonstrate, and explain how to pass a moving ball under pressure (see page 125).

2. Practice passing a moving ball under pressure.

Description

Groups of four—Form groups of four by telling the pairs of players from game 1 to join to make groups of four. Practice team passing using one or more of these three variations, depending on the abilities of your players (see variations):

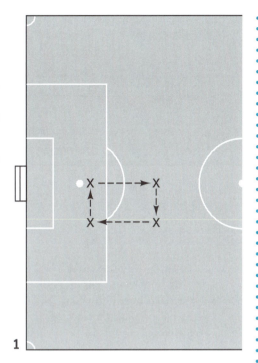

1. Pass the ball in a square, stopping the ball before passing.

2. Keep passing the moving ball in a continuous relay (pass and follow the ball).

3. Mark square areas with cones. Have three players in each square try to keep the ball away from one defender. Switch who plays the defender every six passes or three minutes.

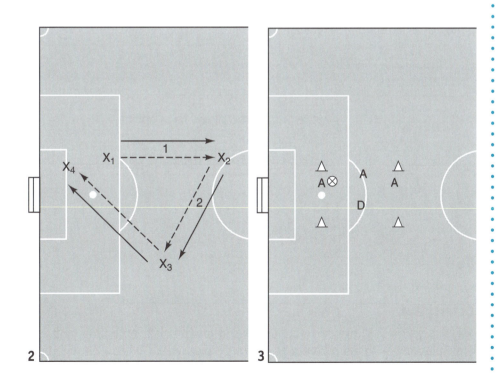

COACH's cues

"Receive the pass and push it toward your target."

"Get close to the ball."

"Face the receiver."

"Point the toe outward." (Use the inside of the foot to pass.)

"Defender, try to get the ball." (Use in the third variation of skill practice 1 only.)

Skill Practice 2 (10 minutes)

1. Introduce, demonstrate, and explain how to use passing and support to move the ball forward (see pages 123–124 and 125–127).

2. Practice combining passing and support to move the ball forward.

Description

3 v 1—Each team of three gets the ball from one end of the field to the other without running with the ball (by passing). One player is a defender.

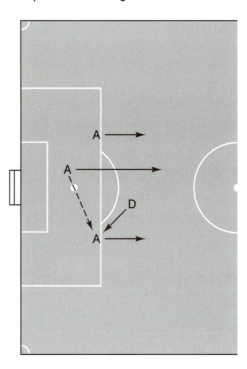

COACH's cues

"Move to a good place to support."

"Pass and move."

"Defender, try to get the ball."

Game 2 (10 minutes)

Goal

Players will learn to pass in the game.

Description

4 v 1, 4 v 2, 4 v 3, or 4 v 4 (choose based on the skill proficiency of your players)—Rotate players accordingly so they all have a chance to play offense and defense. (See chapter 4 for more on the use of lopsided games.) Teams try to pass often.

Practice 3

COACH's cue

"Pass and support."

COACH's point

☞ The first touch, when the player first receives the ball, is extremely important when passing and receiving a ball under pressure. Encourage players to use the inside or the outside of the foot with their first touch to set the ball rolling in the direction they want to pass next.

Team Circle (5 minutes)

Key Idea: Responsibility

Gather children into a group between two cones about 10 feet apart. Stand in the middle of the circle with a ball. "I'm going to show you two different ways to handle the same situation. Think about which is the best way to handle this." Choose a player to receive a pass from you. Make a bad pass and then stomp angrily away from the group. Retrieve the ball and make another bad pass. This time, run to get the ball and make a pass that goes directly to the player. "If you think the first response is the way to handle making a bad pass, stand next to this cone. If you think the second way is better, stand next to this one." Ask players to explain their choices. "It's important to be a good sport in soccer." Highlight how and why. "That's being responsible to your teammates."

Wrap-Up

Make summary comments about practice. Remind them of the next practice day and time, and give them a sneak preview of that practice: trapping the ball.

Variations

Skill practice 1 has three levels of difficulty. You may choose to do all three in sequence, begin with level 2, go straight to level 3, or skip level 2. This will, of course, depend on the abilities of your players. If you use all three levels, you may not have time for skill practice 2.

Practice 4

PURPOSE

To keep possession of the ball in the game, focusing on receiving in the game. The objective is to be able to receive the ball under pressure during the 4 v 4 game.

Equipment

☑ One soccer ball per pair

☑ Two portable goals (8 feet by 4 feet) or two pairs of cones per eight players

☑ One cone (or other marker) per player (if possible)

☑ Different colored vests or shirts to differentiate teams

Warm-Up (5 minutes)

Pairs—Partners practice passing (as in practice 2, skill practice 1), pass and move.

Fitness Circle (5 minutes)

Key Idea: Cardiorespiratory fitness

Gather children into a group. "Everyone put your hand up in front of you and make a fist. What did we pretend our fist was at the last practice?" Wait for response (the heart). "What does our heart do?" Wait for response (pumps blood). "Everybody open and close your fist. Put your hands over your chest and feel what's happening. Now, let's run to the goal and back. Will our fist beat faster or slower?" Listen to responses (faster). "Put your hands over your chest. Is it faster or slower moving? When you run during soccer, your heart beats faster, just like the fist opening and closing, and your lungs breathe faster. They slow down when you slow down. Making your heart beat faster helps to improve your cardiorespiratory fitness."

Game 1 (10 minutes)

Goal

Players will learn to pass and support each other in the game.

Description

4 v 4—Each team tries to pass frequently.

COACH's cue

"Pass and move."

Coach: When the ball comes to you, what should you do?
Players: Stop it.

Coach: Then what?
Players: Dribble or get ready to pass or shoot.

Coach: If you want to pass to the right, where should your first touch move the ball?
Players: To the right.

Coach: What about if you want to pass or dribble to the left?
Players: The first touch should go left.

Skill Practice 1 (10 minutes)

1. Introduce, demonstrate, and explain how to receive the ball quickly and efficiently (see page 128).

2. Practice receiving the ball quickly and efficiently.

Description

Pairs—Partners stay 5 to 10 yards apart and pass the ball back and forth.

COACH's cues

"Get behind the ball."
"Use the inside (or outside) of the foot."
"Push the ball in the direction you want it to go."

Skill Practice 2 (10 minutes)

1. Introduce, demonstrate, and explain how to receive a moving ball and direct it toward the goal (see page 129).

2. Practice receiving a moving ball and directing it toward the goal.

Description

Pairs—One partner (or you) feeds the ball to the other player, who controls the moving ball, dribbles, and shoots into the goal.

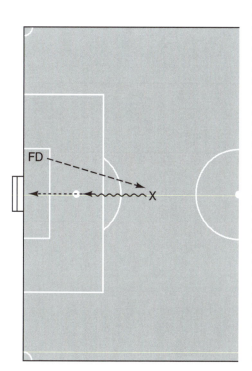

FD

X

COACH's cues

"Use the inside (or outside) of the foot."
"Push the ball toward the goal."
"Dribble and shoot."

Game 2 (15 minutes)

Goal

Players will learn to receive passes effectively under pressure in the game.

Description

4 v 1, 4 v 2, 4 v 3, or 4 v 4 (choose based on the skill proficiency of your players)—Rotate players accordingly so they all have a chance to play offense and defense. Each team tries to pass frequently and to leave one player forward.

COACH's cue

"Control and pass."

Practice 4

Team Circle (5 minutes)

Key Idea: Honesty

Gather children into a group near two cones about 10 feet apart. "What is a foul?" Listen to their responses. Choose a player to help demonstrate responses (include hand balls, bumping players, and kicking or tripping). "Should you admit to a foul if no official sees it? Those who think yes, stand at this cone. Those who think no, stand at this one." Wait for children to choose. "When you know you've fouled, you should raise your hand. You should never take unfair advantage of other players. Can you think of other ways honesty is practiced on the field?" Listen to responses and discuss. "All of those show honesty."

Wrap-Up

Make summary comments about practice. Remind them of the next practice day and time, and give them a sneak preview of that practice—attacking as a team.

Variations

You can make skill practice 2 more difficult for better players by providing some mild pressure as players receive the ball. Then the player must beat you before shooting at the goal.

COACH's point

☞ Continue to emphasize good support of teammates by having teams designate a forward who stays in the attacking half of the field. This ensures that teams play with some depth, as otherwise it is common to see young players continually coming back to the ball. For now, it's best to encourage a forward player by saying, "Stay up there, because if you come back here there's no one to pass to up there." Remember to rotate the forward during game play.

Practice 5

Warm-Up (5 minutes)

Pass and move in teams of four over the field. Each team of four stays close together and moves anywhere on the field, passing the ball among the team members.

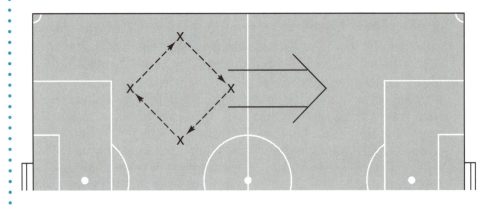

COACH's cue

"Paint the field." (Pretend that the ball is a paint brush and paint the field by passing and moving all over the field.)

Fitness Circle (5 minutes)

Key Idea: Cardiorespiratory fitness

Gather children into a group. "Everyone find your own space. Put your fist up in front of you. We pretend our fist is our . . ." Wait for response (heart). "The heart does what things?" Wait for responses (pumps blood and beats faster when we run or move faster). "When I say, 'go,' everyone run in your own space and make your fist open and close faster at the same time. When I say 'stop,' stop as fast as you can." Begin. "When you run, your heart beats faster. Every time your heart beats faster, it gets stronger because it's a muscle. Muscles get stronger when you use them. Soccer is a great way to keep your heart healthy and strong and improve your cardiorespiratory fitness."

Practice 5

Game 1 (10 minutes)

Goal

Players will learn to spread out ahead of the ball.

Description

4 v 4

Coach: If you don't have the ball, where can you go to help your team move toward the goal with the ball?
Players: Move forward.

Coach: Is it a good idea to leave a player forward?
Players: Yes.

"Have a forward."

Skill Practice 1 (10 minutes)

1. Introduce, demonstrate, and explain how to support ahead of the ball (see pages 121–123).

2. Practice supporting ahead of the ball.

Description

Teams of four, unopposed—Each team passes and moves to the end of the field. The team must make four passes before shooting.

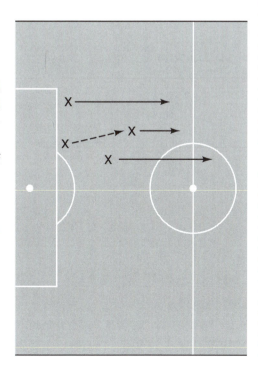

COACH's cue

"Pass and move ahead."

COACH's point

☞ In skill practices 1 and 2 you might see two players go to the same place to receive a pass. Emphasize forming a diamond shape as a way of best using the available space to bring the ball forward. Freeze the practices occasionally to demonstrate.

Skill Practice 2 (10 minutes)

1. Introduce, demonstrate, and explain how to move the ball forward under pressure (see pages 122–123).
2. Practice moving the ball forward under pressure.

Description

Teams of four—Each team passes and moves to the end of the field as you oppose them. The team must make four passes before shooting.

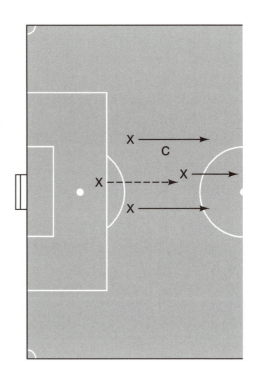

COACH's cues

"Pass and move ahead."
"Move to where you can receive a pass" (away from the defender).

Game 2 (15 minutes)

Goal

Players will learn to move the ball forward as a team.

Description

4 v 1, 4 v 2, 4 v 3, or 4 v 4 (choose based on the skill proficiency of your players)—Rotate players accordingly so they all have a chance to play offense and defense.

Practice 5

COACH's cue

"Pass and move."

Team Circle
(5 minutes)

Key Idea: Responsibility

Gather children into a group near two cones about 10 feet apart. Choose two players to help role play. Set up a triangle of you and the two players. Let the children know you are role playing with them. All three of you take turns passing. When it's your turn, miss the pass and role play yourself as a player: "I couldn't get that pass! It was your fault—you made a bad pass!" Now as coach: "I want you to think about players who make excuses and blame others for their mistakes. Stand at this cone if you think it's okay to make excuses when you make mistakes. Stand at this cone if you think you should try to learn and work harder to improve." Ask players about their choices. "Not making excuses is taking responsibility for yourself."

Wrap-Up

Make summary comments about practice. Remind them of the next practice day and time, and give them a sneak preview of that practice—dribbling under pressure.

Variations

Again, apply greater pressure to the stronger players as they receive the ball.

Practice 6

👉 PURPOSE

Keep possession of the ball and attack in the game, focusing on passing, receiving, dribbling under pressure, and pushing and running. (To push and run, the player with the ball kicks it past the defender—pushes—and runs after it. The defender will have to turn around, which slows him or her down.) The objective is for players to be able to pass, receive, and move the ball forward under pressure during the 4 v 4 game.

Equipment

- ☑ One soccer ball per pair
- ☑ Two portable goals (8 feet by 4 feet) or two pairs of cones per eight players
- ☑ One cone (or other marker) per player (if possible)
- ☑ Different colored vests or shirts to differentiate teams
- ☑ A rubber band

Warm-Up (5 minutes)

Repeat the third variation of skill practice 1 from practice 3.

Fitness Circle (5 minutes)

Key Idea: Flexibility

Gather children into a group. Show them a rubber band. "Let's pretend this rubber band is one of your muscles. See how it moves back and forth, stretching and moving. Let's move our bodies just like the rubber band. Reach and stretch up and down. It's important to stretch slowly without bouncing or jerking." Have them continue for one minute. "Our muscles help us to move and stretch. We need to stretch muscles to keep them flexible and able to move easily. When muscles can move easily, they don't get injured."

Game 1 (10 minutes)

Goal

Players will learn to attack the goal with the ball.

Description

4 v 4

COACH's cue

"Run past an opponent with the ball if you can."

Practice 6

Coach: What are some ways to get past a defender with the ball?
Players: Dribble. Kick it past and run after it.

Skill Practice 1 (10 minutes)

1. Introduce, demonstrate, and explain how to attack a goal under pressure (see pages 128–129).
2. Practice the skill.

Goal

Players will learn to attack a goal under pressure.

Description

1 v 1—Place cones about 15 yards apart. Each player attacks the other player's cone. Player 1 starts by passing the ball to player 2, who then becomes the attacker. Player 1 becomes the defender.

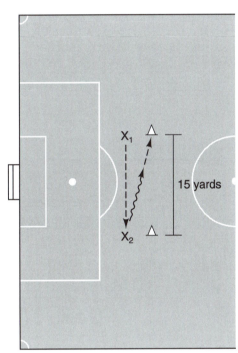

X_1

X_2

15 yards

COACH's cues

"Receive and push the ball into space."
"Push and run past the defender."

Skill Practice 2 (10 minutes)

1. Introduce, demonstrate, and explain how to attack with the ball (see pages 128–129).
2. Practice working together as a team to attack with the ball.

Description

2 v 2 in 30 yards by 20 yards— Reposition the cones from game 1. Have the 1 v 1 pairs from skill practice 1 combine with another pair to make 2 v 2 groups.

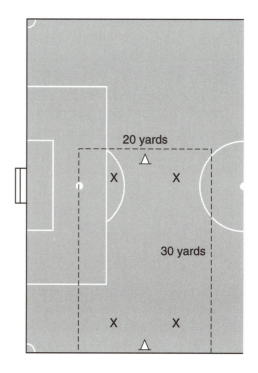

20 yards

30 yards

COACH's cues

"Stay spread out." (This isolates the defender, leaving space behind him or her for the push and run.)

"Push and run by the defender."

Game 2 (15 minutes)

Goal

Players will learn how to attack the goal with the ball under pressure.

Description

4 v 1, 4 v 2, 4 v 3, or 4 v 4 (choose based on the skill proficiency of your players)—Rotate players accordingly so they all have a chance to play offense and defense.

COACH's cues

"Pass if you need to."

"Look for space behind the defender."

"Push and run."

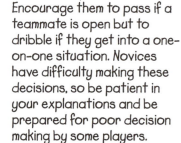

COACH's point

☞ Game 2 focuses on getting players to make a good decision about whether to pass or dribble. Encourage them to pass if a teammate is open but to dribble if they get into a one-on-one situation. Novices have difficulty making these decisions, so be patient in your explanations and be prepared for poor decision making by some players.

Practice 6

Team Circle
(5 minutes)

Key Idea: Caring

Gather children into a circle. Stand in the middle of the circle with a ball. Choose two children to pass the ball with you. "We're going to work on our passing skills." Pass repeatedly to them and not the others. "Tell me how you felt to have only two players get the passes." Listen to their responses. "Sharing the ball and not distracting your teammates shows you care about them. What other things can you do to show you care about your teammates?" Their responses should include encouragement, positive comments for good play, forgiving players that make mistakes, and so on. "Good. Those are all ways you can show you care."

Wrap-Up

Make summary comments about practice. Remind them of the next practice day and time, and give them a sneak preview of that practice—shooting at the goal.

Variations

Encourage better players to use alternative ways, other than push and run, to beat the defender. These could include faking a shot or passing the ball to one side of the defender and running around the other side.

Practice 7

PURPOSE

To attack the goal in the game, focusing on shooting with good technique under pressure. The objective is for players to be able to shoot under pressure using appropriate technique during the 4 v 4 game.

Equipment

- ✓ One soccer ball per pair
- ✓ Two portable goals (8 feet by 4 feet) or two pairs of cones per eight players
- ✓ One cone (or other marker) per player (if possible)
- ✓ Different colored vests or shirts to differentiate teams

Warm-Up (10 minutes)

Repeat skill practice 1 from practice 6.

Fitness Circle (5 minutes)

Key Idea: Muscular strength and endurance

Gather children into a group. "Okay, everyone get down on the ground and do the crab walk." Continue for 30 seconds to one minute. "Are your arms and legs getting tired? You used many of your arm and leg muscles to do the crab walk. What part of the body do you use the most for soccer? That's right—your legs. The more you practice soccer, the stronger your leg muscles will get. Then your legs can keep going much longer before they get too tired. What things can we do to get our legs stronger for soccer?" Let them answer running and kicking. "Right. Now pretend you have a soccer ball in front of you. Pretend to kick the ball in your spot." Have children kick for five counts. "Practicing kicking helps make your legs stronger."

Game 1 (10 minutes)

Goal

Players will learn the importance of having a shooting attitude. (If you don't shoot, you won't score!)

Description

4 v 4

COACH's cue

"Shoot to score."

Practice 1

Coach: What do you have to do if you want to score?
Players: Shoot.

Coach: Where should you shoot?
Players: At the goal. The whole goal is the target.

Skill Practice 1 (5 minutes)

1. Introduce, demonstrate, and explain how to shoot correctly (see pages 128–129).

2. Practice shooting with correct technique.

Description

Groups of four—Keep the same teams from game 1. Each player shoots in turn and retrieves his or her ball (or you can designate someone to retrieve the balls from behind the goal).

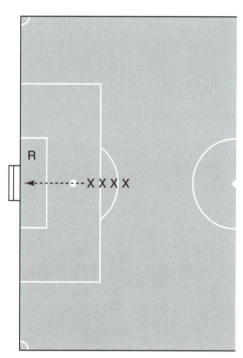

COACH's cues

"Take a long step to the ball." (The step looks like a jump. This helps get the shooting leg back.)
"Get close to the ball." (Keep the nonstriking foot alongside.)
"Use the laces of the shoe." (This provides power.)
"Keep the toe down." (This keeps the ball down.)

Skill Practice 2
(5 minutes)

1. Introduce, demonstrate, and explain how to move onto a rolling ball and shoot (see pages 128–129).

Description

Groups of four—Same as skill practice 1, but a player (or you) rolls the ball forward before each player shoots.

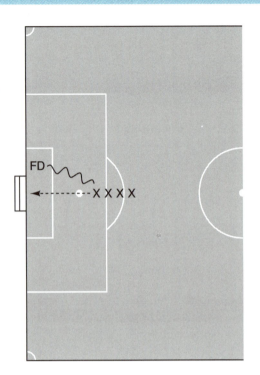

COACH's cues

"Attack the ball."

"Take a long step to the ball." (The step looks like a jump. This helps get the shooting leg back.)

"Get close to the ball." (Keep the nonstriking foot alongside.)

"Use the laces of the shoe." (This provides power.)

"Keep the toe down." (This keeps the ball down.)

Practice 1

Skill Practice 3 (10 minutes)

1. Introduce, demonstrate, and explain how to receive a pass under control and shoot (see pages 128–129).
2. Practice the skill.

Goal

Players will learn to receive a pass under control and shoot.

Description

Groups of four—Same as skill practice 1, but a player (or you) passes the ball before each player shoots.

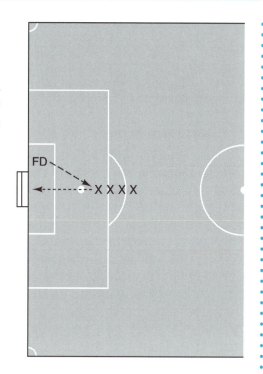

COACH's cues

"Good first touch."(You might have to explain again that they need to set up the shot with the first touch.)

"Control and shoot at the goal."

Game 2 (10 minutes)

Goal

Players will learn to shoot under pressure in the game.

Description

4 v 1, 4 v 2, 4 v 3, or 4 v 4 (choose based on the skill proficiency of your players)—Rotate players accordingly so they all have a chance to play offense and defense.

COACH's cues

"Control the ball."
"Shoot to score."

Team Circle (5 minutes)

Key Idea: Responsibility

Gather children into a circle. "I want everyone to run in a circle, following the person in front of you, without bumping into each other. Keep a space about as long as a bicycle between you, and don't go ahead of the person in front of you." Encourage children to run slowly enough to do all the directions. Continue activity for one minute. "Everyone stop. Did you bump into each other? Did anyone get upset with the person in front of you? You kept your body under control by not going ahead of the person in front of you. You kept your emotions under control by not getting upset with the person ahead of you—he or she couldn't move any faster since you were all running in a circle as a group. Everyone can stay safe and learn when everyone is responsible for himself or herself."

Wrap-Up

Make summary comments about practice. Remind them of the next practice day and time, and give them a sneak preview of that practice—marking or guarding your opponents.

Variations

- Have higher-ability players practice shooting with both feet. (Not all players will be capable of this.)
- Higher-ability players can adapt skill practice 3 by doing their own passing and then, having passed, becoming the defender who chases after the shooter. The shooter must shoot before the defender gets to him or her.

COACH's point

☞ Encourage players to think of the whole goal as the target, even though some players will try to shoot for the corners of the net. Shooting at the whole goal enables them to get more shots on target, giving them a greater likelihood of scoring.

☞ Players can perform skill practices 1 through 3 either with a portable goal or with cones set up in a line to create the required number of goals next to each other.

☞ Higher-ability players will be able to feed each other in skill practices 2 and 3, but you will have to feed the ball to many players. In skill practice 3, pass the ball so the receiver must change the ball's direction before shooting.

Practice 8

Warm-Up (5 minutes)

Players dribble and follow the leader in groups of two or four.

Fitness Circle (5 minutes)

Key Idea: General fitness

Gather children into a circle. "What do our bodies need to do every day to keep going?" Wait for their responses. Discuss sleeping and resting, eating, and doing regular activities. "There's one more thing that's really important—being active and exercising. Let's pretend it's a day that you do not have soccer practice. Your body needs to move every day. With no soccer today, what should we do to move our bodies?" Wait for their responses. If a child suggests biking or swimming, have everyone act out that activity. Act out three activities. "It's important to be active when you don't have soccer practice. Your body needs to move every day."

☞ **PUR...**

To defend your space in the game, focusing on marking and pressure. The objective is for players to be able to defend space by marking an opponent during the 4 v 4 game.

Equipment

☑ One soccer ball per team

☑ Two portable goals (8 feet by 4 feet) or two pairs of cones per eight players

☑ One cone (or other marker) per pair

☑ Different colored vests or shirts to differentiate teams

Game 1 (10 minutes)

Goal

Players will think about defending space and their goal.

Description

2 v 2 to small goal

Coach: How can you stop the other team from getting the ball? (You may need to set this up by saying "How can Katie make it harder for Matthew to get a pass from Michael?")
Players: Stay close to them, mark them. *Marking* means guarding your opponent.

Skill Practice 1 (10 minutes)

1. Introduce, demonstrate, and explain how to defend behind an opponent (see page 130).
2. Practice defending behind an opponent.

Description

1 v 1 with two feeders—One player is the attacker and one is the defender. The feeders are at two cones about 20 yards apart. Feeder 1 passes to the attacker, who must turn and pass to feeder 2. The defender has to stop this.

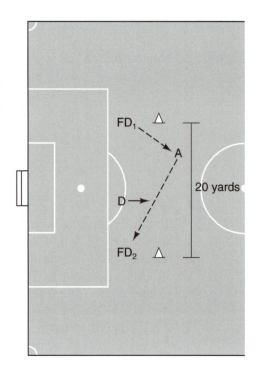

COACH's cues

For the defender

"Stay behind the attacker."
"Stay close."

Skill Practice 2 (10 minutes)

1. Introduce, demonstrate, and explain how to mark an opponent during game play (see page 130).
2. Practice marking an opponent during game play.

Description

2 v 2 to small goal

COACH's cues

"Pick a player to mark." (This is one-on-one marking.)
"Stay with him or her."

Practice 8

Game 2 (15 minutes)

Goal

Players will learn to mark an opponent and pressure the ball during game play.

Description

4 v 4

COACH's cues

"Pick a player to mark." (This is one-on-one marking.)
"Stay with him or her."

Team Circle (5 minutes)

Key Idea: Responsibility

Gather children into a circle. Stand in the center of the circle with a ball. Ask children to call to you and raise their hands if they are in a good position for a pass. Dribble the ball inside the circle, but do not pass to anyone. Continue for about one minute. "Did I share the ball with anyone?" Wait for their responses. "Do you think that is good teamwork? What *is* good teamwork?" Listen to their responses. Repeat the activity, but this time pass to players who call and raise their hands. "Teamwork is when all players are working together, not just keeping the ball to themselves. Responsible team members get in position to receive a good pass. They don't always pass to the same person. And they always work hard."

Wrap-Up

Make summary comments about practice. Remind them of the next practice day and time, and give them a sneak preview of that practice—tackling.

Variations

Make it harder for better players to mark in practices 1 and 2 by extending the size of the playing area. This might mean grouping players of similar ability together during practices.

Practice 9

👉 PURPOSE

To defend your space and win the ball in the game, focusing on pressure and tackling. The objective is for the players to be able to challenge the one with the ball and win the tackle during the 4 v 4 game.

Equipment

- ☑ One soccer ball per pair
- ☑ Two portable goals (8 feet by 4 feet) or two pairs of cones per eight players
- ☑ One cone (or other marker) each (if possible)
- ☑ Different colored vests or shirts to differentiate teams

Warm-Up (10 minutes)

Players play 1 v 1 to a small goal or cones.

Fitness Circle (5 minutes)

Key Idea: Healthy habits

Gather children into a circle. "Everyone is going to run in place. Let's start. Pretend that your body is going to run out of energy because you ate too many chips and drank a soda before practice. Start running slower and slower, and now stop! Now let's pretend that you ate a peanut butter sandwich and drank a glass of milk and a glass of water before practice. Let's run in place." Continue for 30 seconds. "See how you're able to run much longer and keep your energy? Eating healthy foods and drinking plenty of water are healthy habits for every day. You should drink water several times a day and drink even more when you're exercising. Also make sure to get enough sleep, exercise, brush your teeth, and say no to alcohol, tobacco, and other drugs. Keep your body healthy!"

Game 1 (10 minutes)

Goal

Players will learn how to mark an opponent and how to apply pressure when that opponent gets the ball.

Description

2 v 2

COACH's cue

"Use one-on-one marking."

112

Practice 9

Coach: When your opponent gets the ball, where should you move to?
Players: Closer to the opponent.

Coach: What should you then try to do?
Players: Win the ball or tackle. *Tackling* is taking the ball away from the ball carrier with your feet.

Skill Practice 1 (5 minutes)

1. Introduce, demonstrate, and explain how to tackle correctly (see pages 130–131).
2. Practice tackling using correct technique.

Description

Pairs—Place a ball between two players. On the count of three, the players trap the ball between them with the insides of their feet. This is a cooperative tackling practice; both players use the same side of the foot to trap the ball.

COACH's cues

"Get close to the ball."
"Point the toe out" (to use the inside of the foot).
"Keep the knee bent and the leg firm."

COACH's point

☞ Skill practice 1 is a cooperative activity aimed at getting players used to timing a tackle. They work together to trap the ball between them. Skill practice 2 is more competitive. You can control the whole practice for the group by using your whistle to start each repetition when the ball is placed in the middle of each pair.

Skill Practice 2 (5 minutes)

1. Introduce, demonstrate, and explain how to tackle and to keep the ball (see pages 130–131).

2. Practice tackling and keeping the ball.

Description

1 v 1—Set up two cones 10 yards apart. Place the ball between two players, each of whom is at a cone. On the whistle, the players attack the ball to see who can win the tackle and take the ball to the opponent's cone.

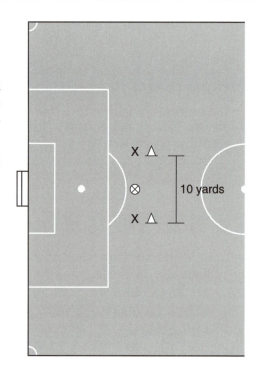

COACH's cues

"Attack the ball."
"Get close to the ball."
"Point the toe out" (to use the inside of the foot).
"Keep the knee bent and the leg firm."
"Control the ball."

Game 2 (20 minutes)

Goal

Players will learn to mark, pressure, and tackle in the game.

Description

4 v 4

COACH's cues

"Mark."
"Pressure."
"Tackle."

Team Circle
(5 minutes)

Key Idea: Caring

Gather children into a group near the goal. Have a ball ready. Ask a child in the group to pass to you. Shoot at the goal and miss completely. Retrieve the ball and make a bad pass. "That shot wasn't very good, was it? How about that pass? . . . Those were mistakes. What should you say to your teammates when they make mistakes?" Listen to their responses. "What could you say to make your teammate feel better? . . . What could you could say to make her feel worse?" Listen to their responses. Have players change the nonsupportive, negative comments to positive ones. "It's very important to forgive mistakes and be understanding of others, just as you would want them to be of you. Making mistakes is part of learning. Saying something that makes your teammates feel better shows you care about them."

Wrap-Up

Make summary comments about practice. Remind them of the next practice day and time, and give them a sneak preview of that practice—defense in a game.

Variations

In skill practice 1, encourage stronger players to make a firm tackle. If both players time it well, they will hear and feel their feet on the ball. This gives them good feedback.

Practice 10

PURPOSE

To defend your space and win the ball in the game, reviewing individual defense (marking, pressure, and tackling). The objective is for players to be able to defend space by marking an opponent and winning the ball during the 4 v 4 game.

Equipment

- ☑ One soccer ball per pair
- ☑ Two portable goals (8 feet by 4 feet) or two pairs of cones per eight players
- ☑ One cone (or other marker) each (if possible)
- ☑ Different colored vests or shirts to differentiate teams

Warm-Up (10 minutes)

Players play 1 v 1 to a small goal or cones.

Fitness Circle (5 minutes)

Key Idea: General fitness

Gather children into a group near two cones about 10 feet apart. Tell them that each cone represents a different food group. "This cone is healthy foods, such as fruits, vegetables, meats, milk, and breads. This other cone is special treat foods, like chips, soda, candy, and sweet snacks. What foods can you eat to keep your body healthy, with enough energy for soccer?" As they respond, have them stand near the cone they choose. "It is important to eat more healthy foods, they give you more energy for soccer and help you grow. Special treat foods should be eaten in small amounts. Can you tell me other examples of healthy foods and special treat foods?"

Game 1 (10 minutes)

Goal

Players will learn to execute good one-on-one defense close to their own goal.

Description

2 v 2 to a small goal or cones

COACH's cues

"Mark."
"Pressure."
"Tackle."

Practice 10

Coach: What should you do when your opponent gets close to your goal?
Players: Get close to the opponent so you can challenge for the ball.

Skill Practice (15 minutes)

1. Introduce, demonstrate, and explain how to pressure the ball and tackle when defending (see pages 130–131).
2. Practice pressuring the ball and tackling when defending.

Description

1 v 1 (plus feeder and collector)—Use one player per team to retrieve balls and one player to feed balls. The defender starts on the goal line with an attacker about 20 yards away. The feeder passes to the attacker, who must try to control the ball before dribbling to the goal. The defender comes quickly off the line to pressure and tackle.

FD

A

D

R

20 yards

COACH's point

☞ Have the feeding done from the side so the feeder is not in the way of the other players. Emphasize that players should stay on their feet while trying to tackle. Some players may lose their footing if they are moving too fast.

COACH's cues

"Go quickly to your opponent."
"Pressure."
"Tackle."

Game 2 (15 minutes)

Goal

Players will learn to mark, pressure, and tackle in the game.

Description

4 v 4

"Mark."
"Pressure."
"Tackle."

Team Circle (5 minutes)

Key Idea: Respect

Gather children into a group. "What have you learned about soccer this season?" Listen to their responses. "What does respect have to do with playing soccer or any sport? It takes many years to master the game of soccer, so soccer deserves your respect. Every year there are new skills to learn and improve on; every year you play, you'll get better. That's why you need to come back next year! What examples of players showing respect have you seen this soccer season?" Listen to their responses and discuss.

Wrap-Up

Make summary comments about what everyone learned over the season. Encourage players to come back next year!

Variations

- In the skill practice, have more advanced players defend against two opponents. The extra player can either be the ball collector or the passer, who then joins in the practice.
- Again in the skill practice, give weaker players a shorter distance to go to reach the attacker.

The Building Blocks

In part II we provided you with the plans for coaching soccer, starting with the season plans for teaching four- through seven-year-olds the basics of soccer. We presented important fitness and character development concepts, then gave detailed plans for conducting each practice session. In part III we'll present more information about how to teach the subject matter planned in part II. In chapter 8 we'll review teaching basic soccer tactics and skills, and in chapter 9 we'll examine the rules of the game, along with a few unwritten traditions that are useful to know. In chapter 10 we'll tell you more about the basic fitness and safety concepts we want you to integrate into your soccer teaching, and in chapter 11 we'll do the same for teaching character development.

The more you understand the subject matter you teach, the better you're likely to teach it. See the information here as a good starting point, but feel free to learn more by exploring resources listed in appendix A at the end of this book.

Teaching Soccer Tactics and Skills

Now we'll give you more in-depth information about the tactics and skills you'll be teaching to your YMCA Rookies players. The tactics and skills that we'll describe for you include team tactics, individual offensive skills, and individual defensive skills. We will illustrate each skill and include suggestions for how to correct common errors in execution.

Team Tactics

The tactics you should teach players to use when their team has the ball are to support each other on the field by using the triangle method, to move continuously during play, to spread out the attack, and to pass and shoot often.

The Triangle Method

Essential to any soccer team's success is how players support their teammates on the field. Teaching them the triangle concept is one way you can reinforce the need to spread out, provide support, and give the dribbler more options. The triangle concept is simply that players should try to maintain a triangle formation on the field, with the dribbler usually at the apex of the triangle (see figure 8.1). The triangle formation is used in sports such as hockey and basketball, ones that require a fluid, dynamic interplay.

Figure 8.1   The triangle formation.

By maintaining a triangle, players will be able to spread out the defense and at the same time provide the player with the ball with more options.

To teach young players proper triangle positioning, use the easiest possible explanation. One method is to position players along the outer edges of the dribbler's field of vision. Players can find these outer edges by swinging both arms from behind the back around to the front until they are just visible.

Moving Continuously

Offensive players are easy to mark if they are inactive. Encourage your players to move continuously to an open area downfield to receive passes. If teammates are not open, the dribbler should move the ball to an open area. This tactic will put pressure on the defense and probably cause a defensive player to leave his or her player, leaving an offensive player open for a pass. When a pass is made, the player to whom the pass was intended should come to meet the ball.

Keep in mind that passing takes teamwork. Often what we consider bad passes are, in fact, good passes that were improperly received. Therefore, if a pass is stolen, don't simply conclude that the passer was at fault; a stolen pass may also result from an exceptional defensive play or poor receiving technique.

Error

Receiver waiting for a pass to arrive when a defender is in the area

Correction

1. Tell players to get in line with the ball.

2. Insist that receivers move to meet the ball (see figure 8.2) while maintaining sufficient control to receive the pass.

Figure 8.2 The receiver should move to meet the ball when defender is in the area.

Spreading Out the Attack

Have your players keep distance between each other on the field. By spreading your offensive attack, your team will open space for dribbling, passing, and scoring opportunities. Bunching together brings more defenders into position to intercept a pass or steal the ball. Also, when offensive players are too close together, one defender can guard more than one player.

Error

Offensive players positioned in a straight line across the field (see figure 8.3)

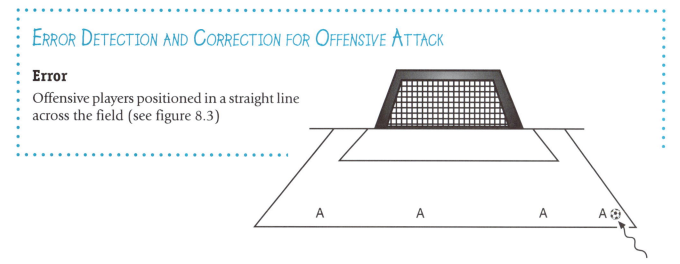

Figure 8.3 Incorrect offensive positioning.

(continued)

123

(continued)

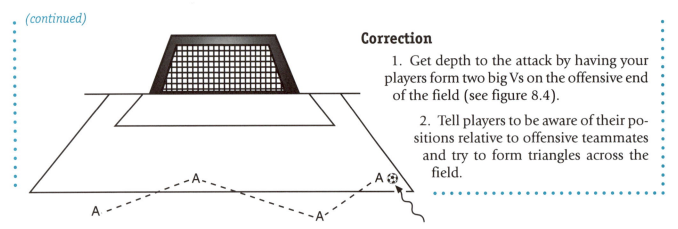

Correction

1. Get depth to the attack by having your players form two big Vs on the offensive end of the field (see figure 8.4).

2. Tell players to be aware of their positions relative to offensive teammates and try to form triangles across the field.

Figure 8.4 Using the V formation adds depth to the offensive attack.

Pass and Shoot Frequently

Quick, frequent passes require the defense to adjust constantly. Also, when defenders are out of position, it is easier to shoot the ball to the goal. The more shots on goal your players take, the greater your team's chances to score, but make sure they're good shots from reasonable distances and angles.

So now that we've looked at team tactics, let's talk about individual skills—offensive and defensive.

Individual Offensive Skills

These are the basic skills that players must learn to participate in the game: dribbling, passing, receiving, and shooting.

Dribbling

The first skill needed to play soccer is dribbling, which is moving and controlling the ball using only the feet. Players can use dribbling to move the ball down the field for a pass or shot, to keep the ball from the opposing team, or to change direction.

Players must be able to use both the insides and outsides of their feet to dribble. To dribble with the inside of the foot, the player turns the foot out, then pushes the ball forward while moving (see figure 8.5). To dribble with the outside of the foot, the player must turn the foot in, then push the ball slightly forward or to the side (see figure 8.6).

Players may have trouble dribbling at first. Have them start by walking and dribbling. Once they can do that, ask them to speed up their dribbling pace. Insist that they look up as they dribble and not down at the ball. If they always look down, they are likely to have the ball stolen by an opponent or may not see a teammate who is open for a pass. Encourage players to use either foot to dribble—this will make it easier for them to protect the ball from opponents.

Figure 8.5 Inside-of-foot dribble.

As your players improve, have them dribble against an opponent. Being marked (guarded) by a defender will require them to vary their speed, change direction, and shield the ball. Have them prepare for defensive pressure by practicing speeding up and slowing down as they dribble and by dribbling around towels or cones.

Here are some keys to dribbling:

◎ Push the ball softly in the desired direction if you are dribbling close to defenders.

◎ Look up and watch for other players.

◎ Keep the ball close to your feet. If it is too far ahead, other players can steal it.

◎ Shield the ball from opponents.

◎ Run at a speed at which you can control the ball.

◎ If you are dribbling fast, push the ball out several feet ahead and sprint to the ball.

Figure 8.6 Outside-of-foot dribble.

ERROR DETECTION AND CORRECTION FOR DRIBBLING

Error

Letting the ball get too far away to keep possession

Correction

1. Keep the ball underneath the body, close to the feet.

2. Nudge the ball gently in different directions, never letting it get more than a stride's length away.

3. Determine whether the grass or ball require adjustments. A highly inflated ball or extremely short grass will cause the ball to roll faster and farther.

Passing

Passing is another essential skill, as it allows the team to maintain possession of the ball and create scoring opportunities. Passes should be short and crisp; an opposing player is likely to steal long or slow passes. However, players should avoid using passes that are too hard and difficult to control. When passing under pressure, the player should pass, then move into space quickly.

Players should kick short passes with the inside of the foot. Here is the correct technique for short passes:

1. Plant the nonkicking foot alongside and near the ball.

2. Square up the hips and shoulders to the teammate for whom you intend the pass, and turn out the kicking foot (see figure 8.7a).

3. Swing the kicking foot straight at the center of the ball (see figure 8.7b).

4. Follow through by swinging the kicking leg well beyond the point of impact with the ball, in the direction of the teammate to whom you are passing the ball (see figure 8.7c).

a   b   c

Figure 8.7 Proper technique for kicking short passes.

Sometimes a game situation will call for a player to make a long pass to a teammate across the field. The best way to make a long pass is to loft the ball through the air using the top of the foot. This is the correct technique for lofting passes:

1. Plant the nonkicking foot slightly behind and to the side of the ball (see figure 8.8a).

2. Point the toes of the kicking foot down, and kick the ball with the shoe-lace area. Kick under the ball (see figure 8.8b).

3. Watch the kicking foot contact the bottom half of the ball and lift it off the ground (see figure 8.8c).

Figure 8.8 Proper technique for kicking a long pass.

Players should learn to use the outside of the foot to pass to the side, but this technique may be uncomfortable and difficult for them to perform. They also may have difficulty passing with the top of the foot or shoelace area (also called a power pass), as they tend to use their toes instead. Because of these problems, you may want to have young players master the short passes before they learn these other types of passes.

ERROR DETECTION AND CORRECTION FOR PASSING

Error

Lack of accuracy

Correction

1. Plant the nonkicking foot beside the ball with the toes pointed toward the teammate who will receive the pass.

2. Square your shoulders and hips to the receiver (see figure 8.9).

3. Keep the kicking foot firm throughout the kicking motion.

4. Follow through with the kicking foot.

Figure 8.9 Squaring your hips and shoulders to the receiver helps ensure accuracy.

127

Figure 8.10 Receiving with the inside of the foot.

Receiving

An important soccer skill is receiving the ball. A player can receive the ball with just about any part of the body—the foot, the thigh, or the chest. Here are some key components in receiving:

1. Get in front of the ball.

2. Watch the ball.

3. Cushion the ball.

4. Keep the ball near the body.

At the YMCA Rookies level, you will be teaching only receiving with the foot. To receive the ball on or near the ground with the foot, the player should stand in front of the ball and extend a leg and foot out to meet it. After the ball reaches the player's foot, he or she should pull the leg back to slow the ball and relax the foot when the ball makes contact. This technique is called *cushioning* the ball. If a player does not cushion the ball, it will bounce away from the foot and the player will lose control. Receiving with the inside of the foot (see figure 8.10) provides the most surface area and is best for beginning players. Eventually, players should learn how to receive with the outside of both feet.

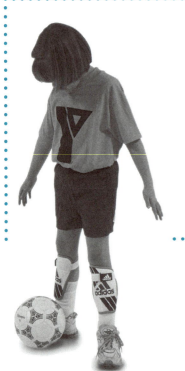

Figure 8.11 Cushioning impact of ball.

ERROR DETECTION AND CORRECTION FOR RECEIVING WITH THE FOOT

Error

Losing control of the ball off the foot

Correction

1. Contact the bottom and side of the ball with the inside of the foot—midway between the heel and toes.

2. Cushion the impact of the ball by moving the foot back to allow the ball to roll in just before the foot makes contact (see figure 8.11).

After receiving a pass, the player should either shoot, pass to another teammate, or push into space toward the goal, dribbling with the ball close. If the player needs to pass under pressure, he or she should do it quickly, with the toe pointed outward.

Shooting

Every player likes to score goals, so your players will be highly motivated to learn proper shooting technique. Point out to them the similarities of shooting and passing; shots also come from the inside, top, and outside of the foot. Also mention some key differences between passing and shooting:

◎ **Length**—Shots often must travel a greater distance than passes because defenders work at keeping offensive players away from the goal.

◎ **Speed**—Shooters frequently kick the ball harder than passers do, so the goalie can't react to stop the shot. Unlike the passer, the shooter doesn't need to be concerned about whether a teammate can control the kick.

◎ **Purpose**—Players take shots for one reason: to score a goal. On the other hand, players pass the ball for many reasons, such as to get a better shot or to keep the ball away from the defense.

At the YMCA Rookies level, instruct your players to shoot using the entire goal as a target. When they are older and more skilled, they will learn to shoot away from the goalie and toward the corners of the goal. Also, tell your players to shoot often. Nothing puts greater pressure on the defense than shots on goal.

ERROR DETECTION AND CORRECTION FOR SHOOTING

Error

Slow and inaccurate shots

Correction

1. Square shoulders and hips to the goal.

2. Take a long step to the ball to cock the kicking leg.

3. Keep the kicking leg cocked until you firmly plant the nonkicking foot beside the ball.

4. Strike the ball forcefully through its center with the foot.

5. Watch the ball as it leaves the kicking foot.

6. Follow through completely, keeping the kicking leg pointing toward the goal well beyond the point of impact (see figure 8.12).

Figure 8.12 The kicking leg should point toward the goal after the point of impact.

When the player is under pressure and receives a moving ball away from the goal, he or she should use both the inside and outside of the foot to dribble toward the goal, then shoot. If the player is under pressure to reach a rolling ball near the goal, he or she should run hard to catch up to the ball and shoot quickly, before it stops rolling.

Now that we've reviewed the main individual offensive skills, let's move to the defensive skills.

Individual Defensive Skills

The two defensive skills your YMCA Rookies players will need to learn are marking and tackling.

Marking

Marking is guarding offensive players to prevent them from scoring. Defenders should try to mark the offensive player to whom they are assigned. They should stay near that player and between the ball and the goal or between the player and the goal (this is called goal side marking). From this position, defensive players will be able to gain possession of the ball off the dribble and intercept passes. Players use marking to slow an opponent and allow teammates to recover to their positions.

A good defensive tactic to teach your players is to get close to their assigned player. This makes it more difficult for their opponent to receive a pass or shoot and gives them a better chance of stealing or blocking the ball if it comes toward their opponent.

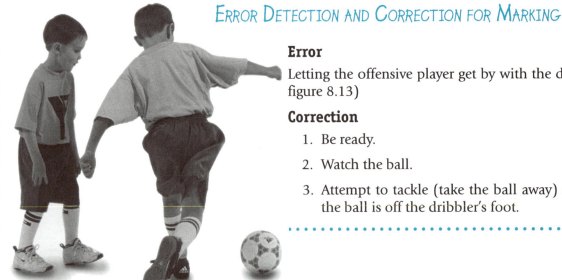

Figure 8.13 Incorrect marking allows the offensive player to get by with the dribble.

ERROR DETECTION AND CORRECTION FOR MARKING

Error

Letting the offensive player get by with the dribble (see figure 8.13)

Correction

1. Be ready.

2. Watch the ball.

3. Attempt to tackle (take the ball away) only when the ball is off the dribbler's foot.

Tackling

Taking the ball from an offensive player is called *tackling*. Players should not be afraid to attempt to take the ball when they have a good opportunity, such as when the dribbler pushes the ball too far ahead. Defenders should, however, be prepared to reestablish position if they are unsuccessful in their takeaway attempts.

Teach players to time their tackles; ideally, they should step in when the attacker temporarily loses control of the ball. Lunging at the ball—or diving in—is a dangerous tactic to teach, even at a young age. A good dribbler will usually go around a defender who lunges at the ball with no trouble. When positioning to make a tackle, the defender should approach the dribbler in a sideways position. If players follow this technique, the attacker cannot push the ball between the defender's legs. Remember, tell your players to go for the ball—not the opponent.

ERROR DETECTION AND CORRECTION FOR TACKLING

Error

Overextending a leg in attempting a tackle

Correction

1. Mark the dribbler as closely as possible and look for an opportunity to take possession of the ball (see figure 8.14a).

2. If the dribbler is careless or unskilled, take advantage by tackling the ball.

3. Gain position by planting the nonkicking leg near the ball (see figure 8.14b). Then use a short, firm kick with the other leg to knock it away from the opponent (see figure 8.14c).

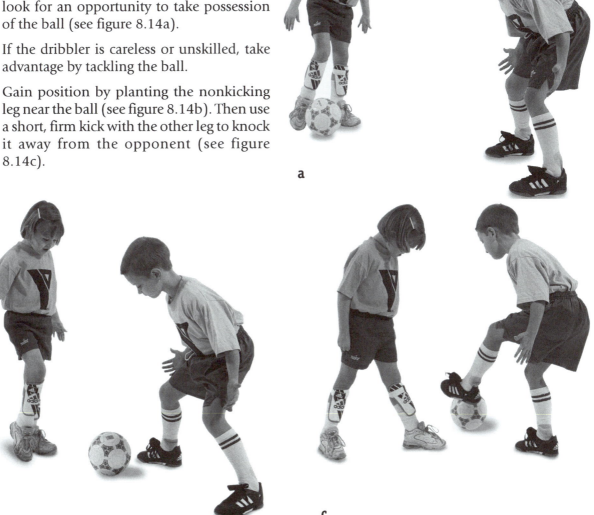

a

b

c

Figure 8.14 Proper technique for tackling.

Teaching Soccer Rules and Traditions

This is where we'll introduce you to some basic rules and traditions of soccer. We won't try to cover all the rules of the game, but will give you what you need to work with children who are four to seven years old. We will explain some rules so you understand the game better; those that you should teach to your players, we have incorporated into the practice plans. We recommend that you use these rules, many of which we have modified from the adult version of the game to make the sport more appropriate for youngsters. In this chapter we'll give you information on equipment, field size, and markings; actions to start and restart the game; fouls; and scoring rules. In a short section we'll show you the officiating signals for soccer. We also will talk briefly about a few unwritten rules or traditions of soccer, those that good players follow to be courteous and safe.

Equipment, Field Size, and Markings

The equipment requirements for soccer are simple: a ball and goals.

◎ Balls come in three sizes: 5, 4, and 3. The size 5 is for adult play, size 4 works well for youth aged 10 to 13, and size 3 is for athletes under 10 years old. The children in the YMCA Rookies program use a size 3 ball.

◎ You can adjust the goals in size depending on the players' ages. The goal for players 12 and older should be 8 feet high and 24 feet wide. For children 8 through 11, the goal should be 6 feet high and 16 feet wide, and for children under 8, the goal should be 4 feet high and 8 feet wide. This is the correct goal size for the children in the YMCA Rookies program.

A full-sized soccer field is 100 to 130 yards long and 50 to 100 yards wide. However, that is much too large for young children. Our recommendation for field size in the YMCA Rookies program is 30 yards long and 20 yards wide for four- to five-year-olds, and 40 yards long and 30 yards wide for six- to seven-year-olds. For some practice activities we suggest even smaller areas.

Figure 9.1 shows the field markings for a soccer field. You will not use most of these markings in YMCA Rookies play; the center circle and spot, the border markings, the corner areas, and the goal areas are probably the only ones you will need to know. (The goal areas should be small, as there is no goalkeeper in YMCA Rookies play. The goal only indicates where to kick.)

YMCA Rookies players need little in the way of playing equipment for themselves. They can wear soccer shoes if they like, but it is not required. Their clothing should be loose fitting and appropriate for the weather. They should purchase and wear shin guards, for safety. If they wear shin guards, they will also have to wear knee-high socks to hold the shin guards in place.

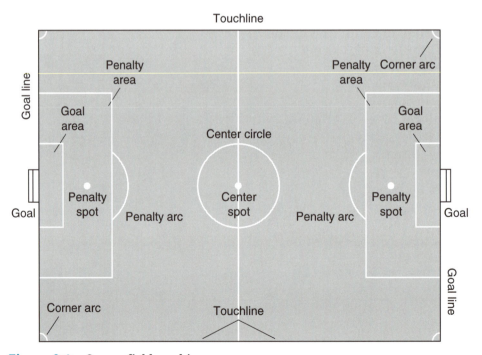

Figure 9.1 Soccer field markings.

Starting and Restarting the Game

Use specific procedures to start a soccer game and to restart it when the ball goes out-of-bounds. Start the game with a center kickoff; restart the game with a goal kick, a corner kick, or a throw-in.

Center Kickoff

Soccer games begin with one team kicking the ball from the center spot. (The team is often chosen by a coin toss.) The opposing team's players are not allowed within the center circle during the kickoff. Players on both teams must be on their half of the field during the kickoff, and the kicked ball must roll forward at least one complete rotation before another player can touch it.

Follow these same procedures after a goal is scored. In this situation, the team that was scored against restarts the game by kicking off from the center spot, and the team that scored stands outside of the center circle in its half of the field.

Goal Kick

When an attacking team kicks the ball out-of-bounds beyond the goal line, as in a missed shot, the opposing team is awarded a free kick called a *goal kick*. The defending team makes this kick, and it must be inside the goal area on the side of the goal where the ball went out of play. The players on the team that kicked the ball out-of-bounds must stay outside the penalty area (see figure 9.2).

Figure 9.2   Goal kick.

135

Corner Kick

If a team kicks the ball beyond its own goal line, the other team is awarded a corner kick from a corner arc. During the kick, defensive players must be at least 10 yards from the player kicking the ball. The kicker's teammates can position themselves anywhere they choose (see figure 9.3).

Figure 9.3   Offensive positioning for a corner kick.

Throw-In

When a player kicks the ball out-of-bounds along the touchline, restart the game at the point the ball went out with a throw-in (see figure 9.4). The team that last touched the ball loses possession, and the other team gets to throw in the ball. The player putting the ball back into play must use both hands to throw the ball and keep both feet on the ground. The player should arch the back as far back as possible to help snap the ball forward. The throwing motion should begin from behind the head and be a continuous forward thrust until he or she releases the ball in front of the head. The throw-in should be put into play quickly, thrown to a player who is not being marked, and passed so it is easy to control.

Figure 9.4   Proper technique for a throw-in.

 **Fouls**

Fouls are called when one player runs into, charges, pushes, trips, kicks, or holds an opposing player. A handball foul is called when a player intentionally touches the ball with his or her hand or arm to gain control.

An offside foul is called when a teammate tries to pass the ball to a player in the offside position. A player is in the offside position when he or she gets closer to the opponent's goal than at least two defensive players (including the goalie). The offside rule prevents offensive players from simply waiting at the goal mouth for an easy shot, but it does not apply to throw-in or corner kick situations. (We won't use this rule in YMCA Rookies play, so don't spend much time explaining it and don't enforce it during play.)

A type of foul you will encounter rarely with YMCA Rookies players is the intentional foul. In regular play, players who intentionally foul or play dangerously are warned once by the official, who presents them with a yellow card. The next time they intentionally foul or play dangerously, they receive a red card and are ejected from the game. Officials also can eject a player without warning if they rule a behavior unacceptable.

Two kinds of kicks can be awarded for fouls, based on where the foul was committed: free kicks or penalty kicks.

Free Kicks

Fouls usually result in either a direct or an indirect free kick. The type of foul committed determines which of the two is awarded (see table 9.1). Direct free kicks can be aimed at the goal, whereas indirect free kicks must touch

TABLE 9.1

Free Kick Fouls

This chart will help you remember which fouls receive a direct or an indirect free kick.

Direct kick	Indirect kick
Handball	Playing dangerously
Kicking an opponent	Obstructing an opponent
Striking an opponent	Goalkeeper taking too many steps (four or more)
Tripping an opponent	Offside
Holding an opponent	
Pushing an opponent	
Jumping at an opponent	
Charging into an opponent	
Charging from behind	

another player before a goal can be scored. The officials signal which type of free kick they have awarded.

At the YMCA Rookies level, we suggest that all free kicks be indirect. This prevents a small child from being hit by a shot.

Penalty Kicks

Penalty kicks are awarded to the attacking team if a defending player commits a direct-kick foul inside the penalty area. A penalty kick is a free shot at the goal by an individual attacker with only the goalkeeper defending against the shot. Penalty kicks are taken 12 yards in front of the center of the goal. The goalkeeper cannot leave the line until after the ball is kicked.

As YMCA Rookies do not use goalkeepers or goal and penalty areas, you probably won't use this rule in YMCA Rookies play. Don't spend much time explaining it and don't enforce it during play.

 ## Scoring

Each time the entire ball crosses the goal line between the goalposts, the offensive team is awarded one goal. Scoring a goal is a thrill for a young child, and it is one tangible way to measure personal performance. However, don't overemphasize goal scoring in assessing a player's contribution. Give equal attention to players who make assists, tackles, or saves, or who demonstrate leadership, sporting behavior, and effort.

 ## Officiating Signals

Even though your YMCA Rookies soccer practices won't be officiated, you may want to use the officiating signals to indicate fouls or out-of-bounds plays. If you use the correct signals, the players will get used to the signals and their meaning. Figures 9.5a-j show some common officiating signals.

 ## Soccer Traditions

Young children need to know only a couple unwritten laws for soccer, and both of those are based on the core values. First, players should raise their hands if they know they've fouled someone. This is especially important in YMCA Rookies games because an official won't be watching. Admitting when you've committed a foul is an example of being honest. Second, players should play cooperatively with those on their team and should show respect to their opponents. This is showing respect for others. They should shake hands with their opponents after the game to thank them for playing hard and providing a good game.

(continued)

Figure 9.5 Officiating signals for *(a)* goal (points to center field for restart), *(b)* penalty kick (points to penalty area), *(c)* corner kick (points to corner area), *(d)* goal kick (points to goal area), *(e)* advantage/play on.

Figure 9.5 *(continued)* Officiating signals for *(f)* official's timeout, *(g)* offside, *(h)* indirect free kick, *(i)* direct free kick, and *(j)* caution or ejection.

chapter 100

Teaching Fitness and Safety

As a coach, you have a great opportunity to teach your players not only about soccer, but also about fitness and health. The attitudes and the knowledge they learn now can be a foundation for their future fitness. You don't have to be a fitness expert to do this. In the practice plans we've supplied you with ideas for discussion in the fitness circles. To give you more background information, we'll discuss some basics of health and fitness in this chapter. We'll begin with the components of fitness and continue with some general training principles and how they relate to fitness. We'll end this section by listing some healthy habits children should develop.

In addition, you are responsible for the safety of your players while they are under your care, so we'll mention some specific precautions you can take. As accidents may happen no matter how careful you are, we'll also list the steps you should take to prepare for injuries to players and describe some first aid procedures for minor injuries and heat illnesses.

We'll conclude the chapter with a brief summary of the legal duties you must fulfill as a coach.

⚽ Components of Fitness

The main components of fitness you need to know about as a YMCA Rookies coach are these:

- ◎ Cardiorespiratory fitness
- ◎ Muscular strength and endurance
- ◎ Flexibility

Cardiorespiratory Fitness

As you might guess from its name, *cardiorespiratory fitness* is fitness of the heart (cardio), the circulatory system, and the lungs (respiratory). It's also known as *aerobic fitness.* Training for cardiorespiratory fitness involves moving large muscle groups, like legs and arms, in a rhythmic activity that is sustained for at least several minutes and uses large amounts of oxygen. Activities such as running, swimming, or bicycling are examples. Such training improves the transportation of oxygen through the blood to working muscles by making the heart and lungs more efficient and the body better able to use the oxygen when it reaches the muscles. Someone who has cardiorespiratory fitness can engage in endurance activities without feeling winded or getting tired easily.

Some concepts about cardiorespiratory fitness that you can communicate to young children are these:

- ◎ Physical activity (such as soccer) is good for fitness.
- ◎ The heart is a muscle that pumps our blood. We can strengthen it by exercise.
- ◎ Our hearts beat faster when we exercise.

Encourage your players to be active at home, whether with soccer or other forms of physical activity.

Muscular Strength and Endurance

Muscles can be fit in two ways. They can be strong, or can have endurance:

◎ **Strength** is the ability of a muscle to exert force against resistance, such as a weight. We use strength to perform everyday tasks such as lifting a grocery bag or opening a door.

◎ **Endurance** is the ability of a muscle to exercise for an extended time without too much fatigue. It's useful in performing tasks that require repeated movements, such as vacuuming a carpet or washing a car.

Muscle strength and endurance can be improved with strength training, but unless you have players who are so unusually weak that they have difficulty playing soccer, strength training is not necessary for children this age. It is more appropriate for older youth who want to train seriously for the sport.

Some concepts related to muscular strength and endurance that your players will be able to understand are these:

◎ We strengthen the leg muscles when we play soccer.

◎ Kicking uses the thigh muscles.

◎ Practicing kicking makes the leg muscles stronger.

Flexibility

Flexibility involves the joints and muscles. It is the ability of the muscles around a joint to allow the joint its full range of motion. Being flexible makes movement easier.

For adults, stretching helps make muscles more flexible. Although it's not known if stretching is effective for children, we do advocate devoting a small amount of time to stretching before and after play. In this way, children learn the proper techniques for stretching, which are as follows:

◎ Warm up with 5 to 10 minutes of low-intensity aerobic activity.

◎ Perform two repetitions of each stretch.

◎ Stretch to the point of a gentle pull, then hold 10 counts without bouncing.

◎ For cooling down, walk around to allow the heart and breathing rates to return to normal. Then perform three to five repetitions of each stretch before the muscles cool.

⚽ Training Principles

You need to know a few principles of training to work with players at this age level:

◎ The warm-up and cool-down principle

◎ The overload principle

◎ The reversibility principle

◎ The specificity principle

Warm-Up and Cool-Down Principle

Before beginning strenuous activity, players should perform some moderate warm-up activity that will increase body temperature, respiration, and heart rate and help prevent muscle and tendon strains and ligament sprains. Warm-up activities could be calisthenics, stretching, or any games with small numbers of players or skill drills that are not strenuous, but include a lot of movement. Use warm-up activities that are interesting to your players.

Once strenuous activity is over, players should slow down gradually with a cool-down activity. Stopping heavy activity abruptly can cause blood to pool in the legs and feet and can slow the removal of waste products created by muscle use. Light activity such as walking or stretching helps to keep blood circulating.

Overload Principle

Luckily for us, our bodies are adaptable. We can present them with a workload a bit higher than what we've done before, and they will, over time, adapt to it. Each time our bodies adapt, we can add more to what we've done before. This is how we can improve our fitness.

We can overload the body in three ways:

◎ **Frequency**—doing an activity more often

◎ **Intensity**—doing an activity harder

◎ **Time**—doing an activity longer

To remember these methods of overloading, think of the acronym FIT. Increasing one or more of these aspects of activity or exercise will put a heavier load on the body.

You can use this principle in all kinds of training. A weight lifter could add more weight as she grows stronger, adding intensity. A runner might add more miles or hours of training, adding time. Either one might choose to exercise more often during the week, increasing the frequency.

Overloading stimulates the body to make changes. Such changes involve the nervous system, which becomes able to recruit more muscle fibers; the circulation, which becomes better at distributing the blood to the working muscles; and the muscles, which produce new protein to meet working demands.

One caution about overloads—don't increase them too quickly, or you could cause injuries. A gradual approach is always safer.

Reversibility Principle

We will state this principle briefly: Use it or lose it! Just as the body can make adaptations when given an overload, it can lose its capabilities when it is not active. It takes three times as long to gain endurance as it does to lose it. If you stayed in bed for a week, you would lose nearly 10 percent of your aerobic fitness. Your strength would also decline, although not as fast. This is why you want to encourage your players to be active, both during and after the soccer season.

Specificity Principle

This principle simply means that the type of training a person chooses to do should relate to his or her goal. For example, bicycling will not improve swimming performance as much as additional swimming will. Performance improves most when the training you do is specific to the desired activity.

 Healthy Habits

One good thing you can do for your players is to instill healthy habits. Being healthy is a lot easier when it becomes a routine part of life. Talk to your players about the benefits of being fit and eating well.

General Fitness

With all the distractions of video games and TV, many children are less active than they might otherwise be. Explain to your players that being active will help them be healthier and feel better. It also may help their soccer game!

Discuss how other good health habits can help them, such as getting enough sleep; brushing their teeth and washing well; and saying no to tobacco, alcohol, and other drugs.

Good Nutrition

Good nutrition is not the first thing most young children think about when they choose foods. At this age, they may not even know which foods are good for them and which are not. You can start to make them aware of which foods will make them healthier and why good nutrition is important.

A simple guide for a good diet is the U.S. Department of Agriculture's food guide pyramid (see figure 10.1). This is a guide that encourages us to eat lots of breads, cereals, rice, pasta, vegetables, and fruits; a smaller amount of meat, cheese, eggs, dried beans, or nuts; and only a little bit of fats, oils, and sweets. Eating this way cuts down on the amount of fats in the diet and helps ensure an adequate amount of vitamins and minerals.

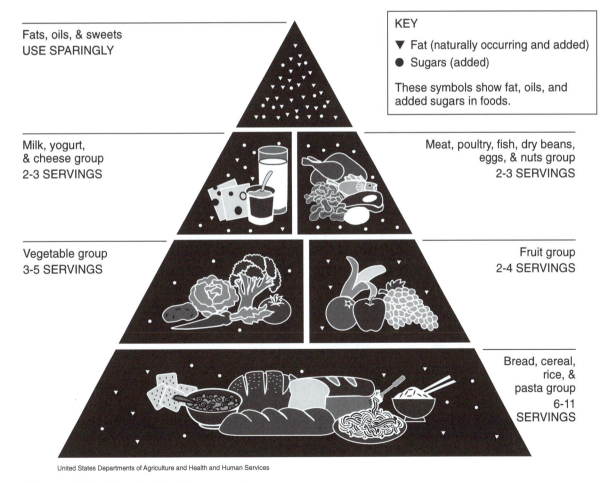

KEY

▼ Fat (naturally occurring and added)

● Sugars (added)

These symbols show fat, oils, and added sugars in foods.

Fats, oils, & sweets
USE SPARINGLY

Milk, yogurt,
& cheese group
2-3 SERVINGS

Meat, poultry, fish, dry beans,
eggs, & nuts group
2-3 SERVINGS

Vegetable group
3-5 SERVINGS

Fruit group
2-4 SERVINGS

Bread, cereal,
rice, &
pasta group
6-11
SERVINGS

United States Departments of Agriculture and Health and Human Services

Figure 10.1   The food guide pyramid.

The following list specifies what one serving is for the foods in these groups:

◎ 1/2 cup of fruit or vegetable

◎ 3/4 cup of juice

◎ One slice of bread

◎ One cup of milk

◎ One average piece of fruit

◎ One cup of salad greens

◎ 1/2 cup of cooked pasta

◎ Lean meat about the size of a deck of cards

According to Kalish (1996), the number of servings children should eat depends on their age, height, weight, and level of physical activity. One exception is milk; children need to have three milk group servings a day.

 ## Safety Precautions

As a coach, you're morally and legally responsible for the safety of your players during practice sessions or games. You need to take some regular precautions to protect their safety. Some simple ways that you can protect your players from harm are a preseason physical exam, regular inspection of equipment and facilities, matching athletes by maturity, warning players and their parents of the potential for injury, supervising properly and keeping good records, and adjusting practices or games according to environmental conditions.

Preseason Physical Examination

We recommend that your players have a physical examination before participating in YMCA Rookies soccer. The exam should address the most likely areas of medical concern and identify youngsters at high risk. We also suggest that you have players' parents or guardians sign a participation agreement form and a release form to allow their children to be treated in case of an emergency. See appendix B, Preparticipation Screening for YMCA Youth Super Sports Programs, for specific information on what should take place during the preseason physical examination.

Regular Inspection of Equipment and Facilities

At the beginning of the season, check the quality and fit of all protective equipment your players use (mainly shin guards for YMCA Rookies soccer players), and inspect the equipment regularly during the season. Ensure that all players have adequate shin guards and that they wear them. Players must replace worn-out, damaged, lost, or outdated equipment immediately.

Remember, also, to examine regularly the field on which your players practice and play. Remove hazards, report conditions you cannot remedy, and request maintenance as necessary. If unsafe conditions exist, either make adaptations to avoid risk to your players' safety or stop the practice or game until safe conditions have been restored.

Matching Athletes by Maturity

Children of the same age may differ in height and weight by up to 6 inches and 50 pounds. That's why, in contact sports or sports in which size provides an advantage, it's essential to match players against opponents of similar size and physical maturity. Such an approach gives smaller, less mature children a better chance to succeed and avoid injury, and it provides larger children with more of a challenge.

Informing Players and Parents of Inherent Risks

You are legally responsible for warning players of the inherent risks involved in playing soccer. Failure to warn is one of the most successful arguments in lawsuits against coaches. Therefore, thoroughly explain the inherent risks of soccer, and make sure each player knows, understands, and appreciates those risks.

The preseason parent orientation program is a good opportunity to explain the risks of the sport to parents and players. It also is an appropriate time to have both the players and their parents sign waivers releasing you from liability should an injury occur. Such waivers do not relieve you of responsibility for your players' well-being, but lawyers recommend them.

Proper Supervision and Record Keeping

With young children, simply being present in the area of play is not enough; you must actively plan and direct team activities and closely observe and evaluate players' participation. You're the watchdog responsible for the players' well-being. So if you notice a player limping or grimacing, give him or her a rest and examine the extent of the injury.

As part of your supervision duties, you are expected to foresee potentially dangerous situations and be in a position to help prevent them from occurring. As a coach, you're required to know and enforce the rules of the sport (especially safety rules), prohibit dangerous horseplay, and hold practice or games only under safe weather conditions (see the next section). These specific supervisory activities will make the play environment safer for your players and will help protect you from liability if a mishap does occur.

As a rule, the more dangerous an activity is, the more closely you should supervise players. This suggests that you need to directly supervise younger, less-experienced players, especially in riskier situations such as when they are learning new skills, are violating rules, or are tired or looking unwell.

For further protection, keep records of your season plans, practice plans, and players' injuries. Season and practice plans come in handy when you need evidence that players have been taught certain skills, whereas accurate, detailed accident report forms offer protection against unfounded lawsuits. Ask for these forms from your YMCA, and hold on to these records for several years so that an old soccer injury of a former player doesn't come back to haunt you.

Environmental Conditions

Most problems due to environmental factors are related to excessive heat or cold, though you should also consider other environmental factors such as severe weather and pollution. Giving a little thought to potential problems and ensuring adequate protection for your players will prevent most serious emergencies related to environmental conditions.

Heat

On hot, humid days the body has difficulty cooling itself. Because the air is already saturated with water vapor (humidity), sweat doesn't evaporate as easily, and the body retains extra heat. Hot, humid environments make athletes prone to heat exhaustion and heatstroke (see more on these in Providing First Aid on pages 153–156). Also, if *you* think it's hot or humid, it's worse on the kids—not just because they're more active, but because youngsters under the age of 12 have a more difficult time than adults regulating their body temperature.

To provide for players' safety in hot or humid conditions, take the following preventive measures:

◎ Monitor weather conditions and adjust practices or games accordingly. Figure 10.2 shows the specific air temperatures and humidity percentages that can be hazardous.

◎ Acclimatize players to exercising in high heat and humidity. Players can make adjustments to high heat and humidity over 7 to 10 days. During this time, hold practices at low to moderate activity levels and give the players water breaks every 20 minutes.

◎ Switch to light clothing. Players should wear shorts and white T-shirts.

◎ Identify and monitor players who are prone to heat illness. Those players who are overweight, heavily muscled, or out of shape will be more prone to heat illness, as will be those who work excessively hard or who have suffered heat illness before. Closely monitor these players and give them water breaks every 15 to 20 minutes.

◎ Make sure players replace water lost through sweat. Encourage your players to drink one liter of water each day, to drink eight ounces of water every 15 minutes during practice or games, and to drink four to eight ounces of water 15 minutes before practice or games.

◎ Replenish electrolytes lost through sweat, such as sodium (salt) and potassium. The best way to replace these nutrients is by eating a healthy diet that contains fresh fruits and vegetables. Bananas are a good source of potassium. The normal American diet contains plenty of salt, so players don't need to go overboard in salting their food to replace lost sodium.

Encourage players to drink plenty of water before, during, and after practice or games. Because water makes up 45 to 65 percent of a youngster's body weight and water weighs about a pound per pint, the loss of even a little bit of water can have severe consequences for the body's systems. It doesn't have to be hot and humid for players to become dehydrated, nor do players have to

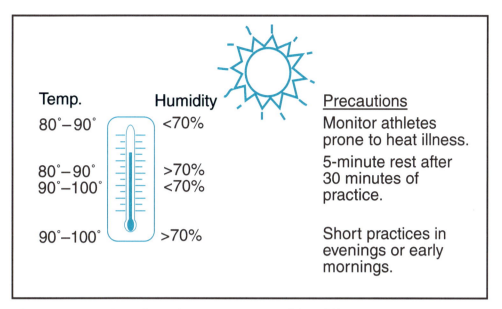

Figure 10.2 Hazardous air temperatures and humidity percentages.

feel thirsty. In fact, by the time they are aware of their thirst, they are long overdue for a drink.

Cold

When a person is exposed to cold weather, the body temperature starts to drop below normal. To counteract this, the body shivers and reduces the blood flow to gain or conserve heat. No matter how effective the body's natural heating mechanism is, however, the body will better withstand cold temperatures if it is prepared to handle them. To reduce the risk of cold-related illnesses, make sure players wear appropriate protective clothing, and keep them active to maintain body heat. Also monitor the windchill (see figure 10.3).

		Temperature (°F)							
	0	5	10	15	20	25	30	35	40
	Flesh may freeze within 1 minute								
40	-55	-45	-35	-30	-20	-15	-5	0	10
35	-50	-40	-35	-30	-20	-10	-5	5	10
30	-50	-40	-30	-25	-20	-10	0	5	10
25	-45	-35	-30	-20	-15	-5	0	10	15
20	-35	-30	-25	-15	-10	0	5	10	20
15	-30	-25	-20	-10	-5	0	10	15	25
10	-20	-15	-10	0	5	10	15	20	30
5	-5	0	5	10	15	20	25	30	35

Wind speed (mph)

Windchill temperature (°F)

Figure 10.3 Wind chill index.

149

Severe Weather

Severe weather refers to a host of potential dangers, including lightning storms, the potential for tornadoes, hail, heavy rains (which can cause injuries by creating sloppy field conditions), and so on.

Lightning is of special concern because it can come up quickly and cause great harm or even death. For each 5-second count from the flash of lightning to the bang of thunder, lightning is one mile away. A flash-bang of 10 seconds means lightning is two miles away; a flash-bang of 15 seconds indicates lightning is three miles away. Stop a practice or competition for the day if lightning is three miles away or less (15 seconds or less from flash to bang).

Safe places in which to take cover when lightning strikes are: fully enclosed metal vehicles with the windows up; enclosed buildings; and low ground (under cover of bushes, if possible). It's *not* safe to be near metallic objects—flagpoles, fences, light poles, metal bleachers, and so on. Also avoid trees, water, and open fields.

Cancel practice or games when under either a tornado watch or warning. If you are playing when a tornado is nearby, you should get players inside a building if possible. If not, lie in a ditch or low-lying area, or crouch near a strong building, and have them use their arms to protect the head and neck.

The keys with severe weather are caution and prudence. Don't try to get that last 10 minutes of practice or a game in if lightning is on the horizon. Don't continue to play in heavy rains. Many storms can strike both quickly and ferociously. Respect the weather and play it safe.

Air Pollution

Poor air quality and smog can present real dangers to your players. Both short- and long-term lung damage are possible from participating in unsafe air. Although it's true that participating in clean air is not possible in many areas, we recommend restricting activity when the air-quality ratings are worse than moderate or when there is a smog alert. Your local health department or air-quality control board can inform you of the air-quality ratings for your area and whether they recommend restricting activities.

Emergency Care

No matter how good and thorough your prevention program, injuries will occur. When an injury does strike, chances are you will be the one in charge. The severity and nature of the injury will determine how actively involved you'll be in treating the injury, but regardless of how serious the injury is, it is your responsibility to know what steps to take. So let's look at how you should prepare to provide basic emergency care to your injured players and how to take appropriate action when a minor injury or heat illness does occur.

Being Prepared

Being prepared to provide basic emergency care involves three steps: being trained in cardiopulmonary resuscitation (CPR) and first aid, having an appropriately stocked first aid kit on hand at practices or games, and having an emergency plan.

CPR and First Aid Training

We recommend that all YMCA Rookies coaches receive CPR and first aid training from a nationally recognized organization (e.g., the National Safety Council, the American Heart Association, the American Red Cross, or the American Sport Education Program). You should be certified based on a practical and written test of knowledge. CPR training should include pediatric and adult basic life support and obstructed airway.

First Aid Kit

Be sure to have a first aid kit available at all practices and games. A well-stocked first aid kit should include the following:

- List of emergency phone numbers
- Change for a pay phone
- Face shield (for rescue breathing and CPR)
- Bandage scissors
- Plastic bags for crushed ice
- Three-inch and four-inch elastic wraps
- Triangular bandages
- Sterile gauze pads—three-inch and four-inch squares
- Saline solution for eyes
- Contact lens case
- Mirror
- Penlight
- Tongue depressors
- Cotton swabs
- Butterfly strips
- Bandage strips in assorted sizes
- Alcohol or peroxide
- Antibacterial soap
- First aid cream or antibacterial ointment
- Petroleum jelly
- Tape adherent and tape remover
- 1-1/2-inch white athletic tape
- Prewrap
- Sterile gauze rolls
- Insect sting kit
- Safety pins

- 1/8-inch, 1/4-inch, and 1/2-inch foam rubber
- Disposable surgical gloves
- Thermometer

Emergency Plan

An emergency plan is the final step in preparing to take appropriate action for severe or serious injuries. The plan calls for three steps:

1. Evaluate the injured player. Your CPR and first aid training will guide you here.

2. Call the appropriate medical personnel. If possible, delegate the responsibility of seeking medical help to another calm and responsible adult who is on hand for all practices and games. Write out a list of emergency phone numbers and keep it with you. Include the following phone numbers:

- Rescue unit
- Hospital
- Physician
- Police
- Fire department

Take each player's emergency information card to every practice and game (see appendix C). This information includes who to contact in case of an emergency, what types of medications the player is using, what types of drugs he or she is allergic to, and so on.

Give an emergency response card (see appendix D) to the contact person calling for emergency assistance. This provides the information the contact person needs to convey and will help keep the person calm, knowing that everything he or she needs to communicate is on the card. Also complete an injury report form (see appendix E), and keep it on file for any injury that occurs.

3. Provide first aid. If medical personnel are not on hand at the time of the injury, you should provide first aid care to the extent of your qualifications. Again, although your CPR and first aid training will guide you here, the following are important notes:

- Do not move the injured player if the injury is to the head, neck, or back; if a large joint (ankle, knee, elbow, shoulder) is dislocated; or if the pelvis, a rib, or an arm or leg is fractured.
- Calm the injured player and keep others away from him or her as much as possible.
- Evaluate whether the player's breathing is stopped or irregular, and if necessary, clear the airway with your fingers.
- Administer artificial respiration if breathing has stopped. Administer CPR if the player's circulation has stopped.
- Remain with the player until medical personnel arrive.

Your emergency plan should follow this sequence:

1. Check the player's level of consciousness.

2. Send a contact person to call the appropriate medical personnel and to call the player's parents.

3. Send someone to wait for the rescue team and direct them to the injured player.

4. Assess the injury.

5. Administer first aid.

6. Assist emergency medical personnel in preparing the player for transportation to a medical facility.

7. Appoint someone to go with the player if the parents are not available. This person should be responsible, calm, and familiar with the player. Assistant coaches or parents are best for this job.

8. Complete an injury report form while the incident is fresh in your mind.

Providing First Aid

Proper CPR and first aid training, a well-stocked first aid kit, and an emergency plan help prepare you to take appropriate action when an injury occurs. Next we'll look at how to provide first aid both for minor injuries and for heat illnesses, which can be more serious.

Keep in mind that some injuries are too severe for you to treat: head, neck, and back injuries; fractures; and injuries that cause a player to lose consciousness. In these cases you should follow the emergency plan outlined on pages 152–153. Provide first aid *only to the extent of your qualifications.* Don't play doctor with injuries; sort out minor injuries that you can treat from situations in which you need to call for assistance.

Minor Injuries

Although no injury seems minor to the player who has it, most injuries are neither life-threatening nor severe enough to restrict participation. When such injuries occur, you can take an active role in their initial treatment. Most injuries you will see will be scrapes and cuts, strains and sprains, and bumps and bruises.

Scrapes and Cuts. When one of your players has an open wound, the first thing you should do is put on a pair of disposable surgical gloves or some other effective blood barrier. Don't let a fear of acquired immune deficiency syndrome (AIDS) stop you from helping a bleeding player. You are only at risk if you allow contaminated blood to come in contact with an open wound, so the blood barrier that you wear will protect you. Check with your director or the YMCA of the USA for more information about protecting yourself and your players from AIDS.

Once you are wearing gloves, follow these four steps:

1. Stop the bleeding by applying direct pressure with a clean dressing to the wound and elevating it. The player may be able to apply this pressure

while you put on your gloves. Do not remove the dressing if it becomes soaked with blood. Instead, place an additional dressing on top of the one already in place. If bleeding continues, elevate the injured area above the heart and maintain pressure.

2. Clean the wound thoroughly once you control the bleeding. A good rinsing with a forceful stream of water, and perhaps light scrubbing with soap, will help prevent infection.

3. Protect the wound with sterile gauze or a bandage. If the player continues to participate, apply protective padding over the injured area.

4. Remove the gloves and dispose of them carefully to prevent you or anyone else from coming into contact with blood.

For bloody noses not associated with serious facial injury, have the athlete sit and lean slightly forward. Then pinch the player's nostrils shut. If the bleeding continues after several minutes, or if the player has a history of nosebleeds, seek medical assistance.

Strains and Sprains. The physical demands of playing soccer often result in injury to the muscles or tendons (strains) or to the ligaments (sprains). When your players suffer minor strains or sprains, immediately apply the PRICE method of injury care (see figure 10.4).

P Protect the player and injured body part from further danger or trauma.

R Rest the area to avoid further damage and foster healing.

I Ice the area to reduce swelling and pain.

C Compress the area by securing an ice bag in place with an elastic wrap.

E Elevate the injury above heart level to keep the blood from pooling in the area.

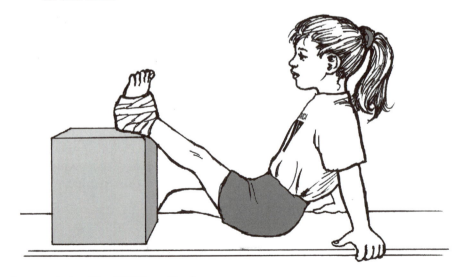

Figure 10.4 The PRICE method.

Bumps and Bruises. Inevitably, soccer players make contact with each other and with the ground. If the force of a body part at impact is great enough, a bump or bruise will result. Many players continue playing with such sore spots, but if the bump or bruise is large and painful, you should act appropriately. Use the PRICE method of injury care and monitor the injury. If swelling, discoloration, and pain have lessened, the player may resume participation with protective padding; if not, a physician should examine the player.

Heat Illnesses

In case your team ever has to play under hot conditions, you should know how to handle two types of heat illnesses: heat exhaustion and heatstroke.

Heat Exhaustion. Heat exhaustion is a shocklike condition caused by dehydration and electrolyte depletion. Symptoms include headache, nausea, dizziness, chills, fatigue, and extreme thirst (see figure 10.5 for heat exhaustion symptoms). Signs include pale, cool, and clammy skin; rapid, weak pulse; loss of coordination; dilated pupils; and profuse sweating (this is a key sign).

A player suffering from heat exhaustion should rest in a cool, shaded area; drink cool water; and have ice applied to the neck, back, or stomach to help cool the body. You may have to administer CPR if necessary or send for emergency medical assistance if the player doesn't recover or his or her condition worsens. Under no conditions should the player return to activity that day or before he or she regains all the weight lost through sweat. If the player had to see a physician, he or she shouldn't return to practice until released by the physician in writing.

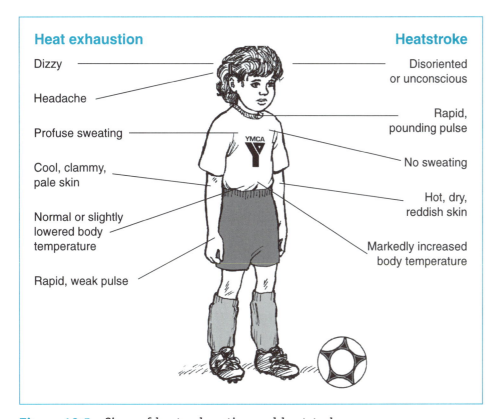

Figure 10.5 Signs of heat exhaustion and heatstroke.

Heatstroke.   Heatstroke is a life-threatening condition in which the body stops sweating and body temperature rises dangerously high. It occurs when dehydration causes a malfunction in the body's temperature control center in the brain. Symptoms include the feeling of being on fire (extremely hot), nausea, confusion, irritability, and fatigue. Signs include hot, dry, and flushed or red skin (this is a key sign); lack of sweat; rapid pulse; rapid breathing; constricted pupils; vomiting; diarrhea; and possibly seizures, unconsciousness, or respiratory or cardiac arrest. See figure 10.5 for heat exhaustion and heatstroke symptoms.

Send for emergency medical assistance immediately and have the player rest in a cool, shaded area. Remove excess clothing and equipment from the player, and cool his or her body with cool, wet towels or by pouring cool water over him or her. Apply ice packs to the armpits, neck, back, stomach, and between the legs. If the player is conscious, have him or her drink cool water. If the player is unconscious, place the player on his or her side to allow fluids and vomit to drain from the mouth.

A player who has suffered heatstroke can't return to practice until he or she is released by a physician in writing.

Legal Liability

When one of your players is injured, naturally your first concern is his or her well-being. Your concern for children, after all, is what made you decide to coach. Unfortunately, you must also consider something else: can you be held liable for the injury?

From a legal standpoint, a coach has nine duties to fulfill. We've discussed all but planning (see chapters 5–7) in this chapter.

1. Provide a safe environment.

2. Properly plan the activity.

3. Provide adequate and proper equipment.

4. Match or equate athletes.

5. Warn of inherent risks in the sport.

6. Supervise the activity closely.

7. Evaluate athletes for injury or incapacitation.

8. Know emergency procedures and first aid.

9. Keep adequate records.

In addition to fulfilling these nine legal duties, you should check your YMCA's insurance coverage and your personal coverage to make sure you are protected from liability.

Teaching Character Development

This final chapter will deal with character development—teaching values to players. At the YMCA, teaching values is as important a part of the soccer program as teaching game skills. As a YMCA coach, you take on the responsibility to help children learn about and use four core values, values that the YMCA has chosen to emphasize: caring, honesty, respect, and responsibility. Here are some ways you can do this:

◎ Communicate to your players that sporting behavior is an important part of the program.

◎ Teach the four values to players so they know what those values mean. Give them examples.

◎ Include the values in each practice session (character development discussions appear in each practice plan).

◎ Consistently model those values in your behavior so players can see what those values look like.

◎ Celebrate those values and hold them up to players as what is right; this helps them learn to believe in the values.

◎ Ask players to practice the values, over and over again.

◎ Consistently reinforce and reward behaviors that support the values, using the specific value word that is relevant: "Juanita, thanks for helping Amy find the ball. That shows caring."

◎ Consistently confront a player whose behavior is inconsistent with the values, but do so in a way that does not devalue him or her.

◎ Be prepared to talk to parents about the character development portion of the soccer program.

Teaching players values takes a somewhat different approach than teaching skills:

◎ First, it requires that you yourself be a good role model. You should set an example with your words and actions.

◎ Second, you need to know at what level your players are capable of understanding and applying values. Younger children do not think about moral decisions in the same way as adults. Children gradually develop the ability to understand values as they grow.

◎ Third, you must learn to identify situations during practice that relate to the four values. Many everyday occurrences provide a chance for you to demonstrate to players that values are relevant to their daily lives.

◎ Finally, you can use the team circle discussions suggested in the practice plans or find activities of your own, ones that emphasize values and make players think about them.

 # Being a Good Role Model

Most of us believe in the YMCA's core values of caring, honesty, respect, and responsibility, but we don't always follow our beliefs. Our character is measured by our behavior. *We* judge ourselves by our good intentions. *Other people* judge us only by our behavior. Consider the following lists of coaching behaviors for each value. We don't mean these to be comprehensive lists, but to get you thinking about what it means, in practical terms, to be a good role model as it applies to these four important values.

Caring

◎ You spend time after practice helping a player learn a skill.

◎ You comfort a player who is dejected after a loss.

◎ You help a player who is stressed manage that stress.

◎ You inform your players of the benefits of good nutrition.

Honesty

◎ You tell a player that she's not executing a skill correctly and you'll help her.

◎ You tell a player when you don't know a rule (but you'll find out).

◎ You tell a player when you make a mistake, such as misinterpreting who instigated minor misbehavior during practice.

◎ You tell your team that you haven't been as physically active in the off-season as you'd like to be, but you're trying to improve.

Respect

◎ You don't blow your cool when players misbehave.

◎ You listen to players attentively when they are talking.

◎ You bring the same energy and enthusiasm for teaching skills to all your players, no matter how skilled they are.

◎ You don't criticize players in front of their teammates.

Responsibility

◎ You show up on time and prepared for all practices and contests.

◎ You provide appropriate first aid for injured players.

◎ You supervise all practice activities closely.

◎ You intervene when players are misbehaving.

Understanding Children's Moral Reasoning

As you work with children on character development, you need to keep in mind how they think about moral questions. They approach such questions much differently than an adult would, and their perspective changes as they grow. One researcher, Kohlberg (Bee 1995; Crain 1992), has developed a set of stages for thinking about moral questions that he believes children move through as they mature.

Children up through the age of nine generally think about moral questions in terms of obedience and punishment. They assume that fixed rules are set by powerful adults who can enforce those rules by punishment. Children are doing right when they obey the rules unquestioningly. Actions are judged by their outcomes, not by the person's intentions.

Moral reasoning for children nine and younger is very black and white. In soccer, you might expect to see children interpret an opponent's personal foul personally—as an intentional attack—when it is most likely unintentional and a result of poor skill or lack of experience.

Around the age of 10, most children think about moral questions in terms of what works best for them. The right thing is the thing that brings pleasant results. They also think about making deals with others—if I do something for you, then you may, in turn, do something for me. Making fair deals is important. A 10- or 11-year-old may agree to congratulate the opponent on good plays or at the end of a game because he or she knows that the behavior pleases most adults and most other kids. However, if the opponent doesn't congratulate his or her good play in return, he or she may stop that behavior because it doesn't generate a pleasant or fair result.

Near 16, most players have started thinking about moral questions in terms of how those questions relate to the expectations of their family and community. The focus is behaving in good ways, having good motives and good feelings toward others. At this point, players also start to consider people's intentions when judging actions.

They can better understand their roles as representatives of their team or their YMCA and as role models for younger players. This is particularly true when their coaches, parents, and teammates encourage them. Such encouragement would be likely to cause them to modify their game behaviors to fulfill others' expectations.

Moving from one type of thinking about morality to another happens gradually and may occur at different ages for different children. However, this gives you some broad guidelines for how most players on your team may look at character development questions when you bring them up in team circles or during practice or games.

Using Teachable Moments

During practices, you may find that a situation arises that gives you a chance to point out how values apply. This type of situation is known as a *teachable moment,* and it might be something like one team's behavior toward an opponent, one player's behavior toward another, or a violation of team rules. Use teachable moments when they occur. Stop a skill practice or game to comment on an incident. Don't do this too frequently, but it can be effective when a good opportunity arises to illustrate a value discussed earlier.

A teachable moment can be triggered by either good or bad actions; you can praise an individual's or group's supportive, fair behavior or stop an activity briefly to talk about negative behavior. Here are some examples:

◎ If one player yells at another for a mistake in play, talk to that player about respect.

◎ If a player does something dangerous during a game, have a brief discussion with that player about responsibility and caring for others.

◎ If a player helps another child who is hurt, praise the player for caring.

◎ If a player raises her hand to admit committing a foul that wasn't called, congratulate her for being honest.

Try to balance positive and negative instances; don't use just negative situations.

Teachable moments are occasions when you can hold up the right value and explain why it is the acceptable thing to do. Doing this illustrates to players what values look like beyond the words and how values are a part of our everyday lives.

⚽ Using Values Activities

We've already included a team circle in each practice plan. This gives you a topic for brief discussion of one or more of the core values. Just as practice drills focus on physical skills, team circles focus on character development. They help players realize that participation in soccer also teaches them about themselves and others.

Here are some tips on leading team circle discussions:

◎ Begin discussions by reviewing the YMCA House Rules: speak for yourself, listen to others, avoid put-downs, take charge of yourself, and show respect. (Repeat this in your first three or four team circles; after that, you'll probably only need to reinforce these House Rules occasionally.)

◎ Be yourself. Children respect an adult who listens to them and who talks honestly.

◎ As a role model for your players, be willing to admit mistakes; it will make players more likely to be open about themselves.

◎ Give players a chance to respond, but allow them to pass if they want to. Reinforce their responses with a nod, smile, or short comment like "Thanks," "OK," "That's interesting," or "I understand." Give the player speaking your undivided attention.

◎ After all players have had a chance to respond to your team circle question, briefly summarize the responses and add your own comments. Try not to lecture.

You might also include activities of your own that reinforce values. The YMCA of the USA has created a number of character development resources; ask your YMCA if they can make those available to you. Here are a few ideas taken from the YMCA Character Development Activity Box (YMCA of the USA, 1997):

◎ Tell your players that one way to demonstrate caring is to do kind things for others. Ask the players to brainstorm ideas of things they could do to be kind to the other members of their families. Some ideas might be washing dishes, cleaning their rooms, or telling a story to a younger brother or sister. Encourage each player to do one kind act for each member of his or her family during the next week, and discuss what they did during the next week's practice.

◎ Point out that on a team, all players must respect their teammates, because they are not a team without every one of them. Divide the team into two equal groups. Have each group line up in single file as fast as they can in the order you tell them to. They can race to see which group can line up the fastest. First, say "I want you to line up from shortest to tallest." After both groups have done that, indicate who won and congratulate both groups. Then say "Now line up by birthday month, with January in the front and December in the back." Next say "Line up by biggest foot to smallest." Finish by saying "OK, everybody have a seat back in the circle." Ask "Now, in that game, who were the most important players: the short ones or the tall ones? That's right, all were equally important. The same is true for when you were born or how big your foot is. The fact is that every person is important on a team and worthy of your respect. Teamwork is when everyone does his or her part, no matter what that is or how much attention it gets."

◎ Discuss with your players the idea of cooperation versus competition. Point out that the other team makes the game possible. Ask the players to brainstorm ways they might show respect to the other team. These might include saying positive things to the opposing players, congratulating them for outstanding plays, and shaking hands at the end of a game. Encourage your players to do these things when they play.

Any activities you use should meet these criteria:

◎ Be age appropriate and developmentally appropriate.

◎ Account for varied personal backgrounds and differing views on values.

◎ Attempt to change players' attitudes as well as actions.

◎ Focus on long-term results.

◎ Be planned and intentional.

◎ Fit logically with what you are doing.

◎ Be positive and constructive, not putting players down.

◎ Be inclusive.

◎ Be meaningful, not trivial or corny.

◎ Be fun!

Finding More Information

 ## Books

Garland, Jim. 1997. *Youth soccer drills.* Champaign, IL: Human Kinetics.

> Provides coaches of players 5 to 12 with progressive drills for optimal learning and fun, and tips for teaching soccer skills appropriately for each stage of development. Features teaching tips and 77 drills.

Luxbacher, Joseph. 1995. *Soccer practice games.* Champaign, IL: Human Kinetics.

> 120 practice games with conditioning exercises, drills, and simulated game experiences. Excellent for teaching skills and for drill ideas.

Luxbacher, Joseph A. 1996. *Soccer: Steps to success.* 2d ed. Champaign, IL: Human Kinetics.

> Offers 10 steps designed to help teen and adult players learn and practice key skills. Features 94 drills and a list of key points to remember when executing each drill.

YMCA of the USA. 1999. *Coaching YMCA Winners soccer.* Champaign, IL: Human Kinetics.

> The second level of YMCA Youth Super Sports, for 8- to13- year-olds.

 ## Videos

Everything you need to know to coach soccer. With Cliff McCrath.

> A comprehensive program for the novice coach.

The games approach to teaching soccer. 1999. From the American Sport Education Program.

Shows an innovative approach to teaching tactics and skills to 8- to 13-year-olds.

Soccer games: For players 5 to 9 and for players 10 and up. From the Soccer Academy.

Two-part video series; each part contains 20 practice games, teaching the basic skills.

Teaching kids soccer. With Bob Gansler.

Covers the basics of soccer, including common errors, and talks about building confidence and avoiding injury.

Organizations

American Youth Soccer Organization
12501 S. Isis Avenue
Hawthorne, CA 90250
(310) 643-6455

Soccer Association for Youth
4050 Executive Park Drive, Suite 100
Cincinnati, OH 45241
(513) 769-3800

United States Soccer Federation
1801-1811 South Prairie Avenue
Chicago, IL 60616
(312) 808-1300

United States Youth Soccer Association
899 Presidential Drive, Suite 117
Richardson, TX 75081
(800) 467-2237

Preparticipation Screening for YMCA Youth Super Sports Programs

⚽ A Statement of the YMCA of the USA Medical Advisory Committee

The YMCA believes in providing a safe experience for all youth participating in YMCA sports programs. Although staff and other program leaders are primarily responsible for the health and safety of the children during training and competition, it is equally important for parents to determine that their children participating in YMCA sports have no medical conditions that would preclude their participation or result in further injury or harm.

The YMCA of the USA Medical Advisory Committee recommends that YMCAs encourage parents of youth participating in YMCA sports programs to have their children screened for the purpose of (1) determining the general health of the child, (2) detecting medical or musculoskeletal conditions that may predispose a child to injury or illness during competition, and (3) detecting potentially life-threatening or disabling conditions that may limit a child's participation. The following 10 questions are particularly important for a physician to ask during a sports preparticipation exam[1]:

1. Have you ever passed out during or after exercise?

2. Have you ever been dizzy during or after exercise?

3. Have you ever had chest pain during or after exercise?

4. Do you get tired more quickly than your friends do during exercise?

5. Have you ever had racing of your heart or skipped heartbeats?

6. Have you ever had high blood pressure or high cholesterol?

7. Have you ever been told you have a heart murmur?

8. Has any family member or relative died of heart problems or a sudden death before age 50?

9. Have you had a severe viral infection (for example, myocarditis or mononucleosis) within the last month?

10. Has a physician ever denied or restricted your participation in sports for any heart problems?

Although not a complete list, these questions address the most likely areas of concern and are helpful in identifying individuals at high risk. A yes answer to any question should result in further evaluation and a discussion between physician and parent about appropriate sport participation for the child.

On the registration form for each youth sports program, there should be a statement requiring a parent's or guardian's signature, indicating that the child has been properly screened and there are no medical conditions or injuries precluding his or her participation in that sport.

---

[1] *Preparticipation Physical Evaluation*, Second Edition, American Academy of Family Physicians, American Academy of Pediatrics, American Medical Society for Sports Medicine, American Orthopaedic Society for Sports Medicine, American Osteopathic Academy of Sports Medicine, 1997.

Emergency Information Card

Athlete's name _____ Age _____
Address _____
Phone _____ S.S.# _____
Sport _____

List two persons to contact in case of emergency:

Parent or guardian's name _____ Home phone _____
Address _____ Work phone _____

Second person's name _____ Home phone _____
Address _____ Work phone _____
Relationship to athlete _____

Insurance co. _____ Policy # _____
Physician's name _____ Phone _____

IMPORTANT

Is your child allergic to any drugs? _____ If so, what? _____
Does your child have any other allergies? (e.g., bee stings, dust) _____
Does your child suffer from _____ asthma, _____ diabetes, or _____ epilepsy? (Check any that apply.)
Is your child on any medication? _____ If so, what? _____

Does your child wear contacts? _____

Is there anything else we should know about your child's health or physical condition? If yes, please explain. _____
_____
_____
_____
_____

Signature _____ Date _____

Emergency Response Card

Information for Emergency Call (be prepared to give this information to the EMS dispatcher)

1. Location _____

   Street address _____

   City or town _____

   Directions (cross streets, landmarks, etc.) _____

   _____

2. Telephone number from which the call is being made _____

3. Caller's name _____

4. What happened _____

   _____

   _____

   _____

   _____

   _____

5. How many persons injured _____

6. Condition of victim(s) _____

7. Help (first aid) being given _____

   Note: Do not hang up first. Let the EMS dispatcher hang up first.

Injury Report

Name of athlete _____

Date _____

Time _____

First aider (name) _____

Cause of injury _____

Type of injury _____

Anatomical area involved _____

Extent of injury _____

First aid administered _____

Other treatment administered _____

_____

Referral action _____

_____

_____

First aider (signature)

Resources and Suggested Readings

American Sport Education Program. 1995. *Coaching youth soccer*. 2d ed. Champaign, IL: Human Kinetics.

Bee, Helen. 1995. *The developing child*. 7th ed. New York: HarperCollins College.

Berk, Laura E. 1998. *Development through the lifespan*. Needham Heights, MA: Allyn & Bacon.

Crain, William. 1992. *Theories of development: Concepts and applications*. 3d ed. Englewood Cliffs, NJ: Prentice Hall.

Flegel, Melinda J. 1997. *Sport first aid*. Updated ed. Champaign, IL: Human Kinetics.

Golding, Lawrence A., Clayton R. Myers, and Wayne E. Sinning. 1989. *Y's way to physical fitness*. 3d ed. Champaign, IL: Human Kinetics.

Humphrey, James H. 1993. *Sports for children: A guide for adults*. Springfield, IL: Charles C Thomas.

Kalish, Susan. 1996. *Your child's fitness: Practical advice for parents*. Champaign, IL: Human Kinetics.

YMCA of the USA. 1990. *YMCA youth fitness program*. Champaign, IL: Human Kinetics.

YMCA of the USA. 1997. *Character development activity box*. Chicago: YMCA of the USA.